London 21-01-2017

To Nicole

I hope that you've enjoyed
Rita Gallo's Competition..

With very best wishes..

Danilo Conulo

4

GROSVENOR SQUARE

THE MENU OF THE ITALIAN EMBASSY IN LONDON

DANILO CORTELLINI

WRITTEN BY RACHEL HEWARD | PHOTOGRAPHY BY MARC BARKER

FOREWORD
H.E. Ambassador Pasquale Terracciano

The food we serve at the embassy is of great significance. The remit of an Ambassador is the establishment of the greatest number of contacts of relevant people in the country, from politics to finance, industry and culture; people from all of these sectors are often invited to discuss business. It is integral to a fruitful discussion to have a good environment, and food and drink (good wine particularly!) are instrumental in this.

The chef in an embassy is important, and I'm very lucky to have Danilo. He plays an important role in giving some added value to the normal hospitality you would extend. He is a great chef; able to convey the idea of cultural traditions in the finest Italian cuisine. His menus reflect the style and way of life in Italy.

I reject the idea that you should scrap traditional instruments of diplomatic activity; such as receptions and gala dinners. It is in human nature to be more open to discussion if you are enjoying some good food and wine.

Danilo and I always discuss menus and he has many ideas for each occasion, offering options that take the guest into great consideration. For example Italians may get more original and regional dishes whereas British or international guests will get something authentic, but it will be more of what they expect from Italian food.

Each Ambassador chooses his staff, starting with the chef. Danilo had worked for my predecessor so usually it would have been custom for him to leave when I took residence. However I fell in love with his style of cooking. He combines different ingredients in a way that is at once complex yet simple in flavour. He has the ability to showcase the flavour of each ingredient, always innovating on traditional patterns. Like in music, his dishes are variations on a theme. And of course his presentation is exceptional.

One feature of Danilo's job is that he has to cook for small parties which might include the president of the republic, and then a couple of nights later he might have to put on a gala dinner or drinks reception for two hundred people. On every occasion, he always offers the best, choosing a menu that is diplomatic, astute, and most importantly, one that truly represents Italian cuisine at its finest.

CONTENTS

COLAZIONI DI LAVORO

Business lunches and dinners

IL PRANZO DELLA DOMENICA

Sunday family lunches

RICEVIMENTI E APERITIVI

Receptions and cocktail parties

TO MY PARENTS,

for teaching me the true value of a shared meal.

TO MY LOVELY GAIA,

for the constant support in every aspect of my life.

ACKNOWLEDGEMENTS

I would like to thank the following people

The Ambassador HE Pasquale Q. Terracciano and
Mrs Karen Terracciano for their support.

The Italian Embassy in London
and all of the staff for always cheering for me.

My team, without their help none of what I have achieved
would have been possible.

Antonio Carluccio and Richard Vines
for their lovely words.

Also thanks to FoodCycle for the amazing job they do for
our communities! Food waste is a shame and overlooked far
too often.

All the sponsors for the help and support of this book and
many other projects.

Good relationships between chefs and producers are the
base for every good kitchen to be successful. Without
someone striving to give us excellent produce, none of us
would be a good chef.

RISO GALLO UK

GRANA PADANO

DELITALIA UK

PROSECCO DOC CONSORTIUM

IMPERIALE D'ABRUZZO

Phil Turner, Paul Cocker, Rachel Heward, Marc Barker and all
the team at Meze Publishing.

Valerio Di Filippo for the Italian pictures and Flora Luna for
the event pictures.

Marina Emms for the transcriptions of most of the recipes.

Domenico Pantone for the Italian transcriptions.

To all the chefs, colleagues and wonderful people I ever came
across during my career. Each and every one of you has made
a mark on the chef I am today and some of you I can proudly
call friends.

And of course to all of my diners; every smile collected after
a meal fills my heart with joy and reminds me of the reason
why I started cooking 15 years ago.

I hope you enjoy this book as much as I have enjoyed writing
it!

Danilo.

"...every smile collected after a meal fills my heart with joy and reminds me of the reason why I started cooking..."

INTRODUCTION

"It's not just about the food; mealtimes are when you're together as a family."

It sounds stereotypical, but I grew up surrounded by homemade food. My home region of Abruzzo is small, but it is rich in culinary tradition. We have the best of both worlds; with the highest mountain in central Italy, Gran Sasso, as well as a coastline and a thriving farming industry.

It wasn't just the landscape that inspired my interests in cooking, though. In my family, the kitchen was where everything happened. As a child I remember hiding under the table and running around the kitchen with my brothers, getting told off by my grandmother for being too loud whilst she made fresh pasta.

Mealtimes were always important, and remain so to me. It's not just about the food; it's a time to be together as a family. Most of the food we ate was homemade and we grew what we could too; mostly courgettes, tomatoes and French beans – it doesn't get more organic than that.

One of my favourite dishes from home is *timballo alla teramana*, which is a bake a bit like a lasagne, but made with scrippelle, which are Italian crêpes. My grandmother made the best version of this, and it is still unrivalled. Another regional delight is *pasta alla chitarra*, which is translated as guitar after the instrument it is made on. It's a lot like spaghetti, but more square and thicker in shape.

The thing I love about Italian cuisine in particular is how fiercely proud each region, and each individual family is of their own version of a dish. Towns rival and families feud all because we're so attached to our own carefully crafted and tweaked recipes.

Both of my parents were in the restaurant business and actually encouraged me not to go down that route because they knew first-hand how hard it can be; how volatile your position is and how long the hours are. They wanted me to go to college and get a more secure job. But it was always something that interested me and the fact that they told me not to, naturally only made me more curious.

"I had to leave my ego at the door..."

One of the first influential people I worked with was Giovanni Rana, who is one of the most famous names for fresh pasta in Italy. At his restaurant he had a pasta selection like no other and I spent a lot of time developing my skills. Because we only made fresh pasta, I spent whole days just making tortellini and ravioli. I must have made millions! It was all day long and I did it for months. You would think this might become tedious, but my love for fresh pasta came from here.

I started travelling across Italy straight after completing culinary school, working in some of the greatest restaurants of the peninsula, including the two Michelin-starred San Domenico in Imola – a place that still holds a piece of my heart. This is where I technically did most of my training, with a brilliant team who welcomed me as part of the family. I was quite young and owner and head chef Valentino Marcattilii, along with his nephew Massimiliano Mascia (now joint owner and head chef) impressed me immeasurably; I count them both as huge influences upon my career.

After this I worked at a two Michelin-starred restaurant in Isola Rizza, near Verona called Perbellini. This place is famous for the patisserie and the selection is humongous. It was absolutely integral in improving my pastry skills.

My first experience as a head chef was in a small and cosy vegetarian restaurant called Esprì in Colonnella. I have to admit, it was here that inspired me to develop an interesting repertoire of vegetarian dishes. For instance the crispy egg with asparagus recipe in this book originated from Esprì.

All of the places I worked at in Italy helped to shape my cooking style, but after a while I decided the time was right to broaden my horizons and go international. I arrived in London in 2010. It was incredibly surreal, especially for the first six months. Going from a two star restaurant in Italy I thought I was prepared, but London is an incredibly competitive environment – yet it was something I appreciated every day. Once here, I was a 'nobody', and it really put me in my place, forcing me to leave my ego at the door. I appreciated simple cooking using the finest ingredients I could get my hands on, and quickly built up great relationships with suppliers – I found that I could actually obtain better produce in London than I could in Italy. After a couple of months I became sous chef of the Dolada restaurant, a fine dining Italian restaurant in Mayfair, and worked for almost two years alongside the executive chef Riccardo de Prà.

Riccardo was the one who taught me why it was essential that you consider the experience as a diner. Gradually my focus shifted from what I could do to show off, to thinking about what the customer really wants. This allowed me to be on the same level as the diners, so I began cooking for them rather than myself. He was a hell of a chef, and very clever.

In 2011 I took the great opportunity of an internship at the famous three Michelin-starred restaurant Alain Ducasse at the Dorchester. This was a game-changer; cooking at its most ingenious. It was a completely new level where the attention to detail was zealous, almost manic. It opened my eyes to exactly where I wanted to be and made me appreciate the difference between real fine dining and the more rustic way of doing things. By starting from the latter and working my way up, I was able to experience the full scale of our multifarious industry.

Following this I had the pleasure of working as chef-de-partie at the inexhaustibly busy, but highly regarded Zafferano restaurant in Knightsbridge, which at the time held a Michelin star (I can't tell you how many plates of pasta I made whilst here!). After a stint here, I was offered the position of head chef at the Italian Embassy in London.

"Food is about trying to recreate that sense of comfort and home."

I started with the former Ambassador in residence, Alain Giorgio Maria Economides, and for a trial shift I had to cook lunch for some hypothetical guests including highly influential titles. I had six hours to create a menu for an audience I had never entertained. Out of four courses, I did two recipes from my time at San Domenico, one of which was the uovo in raviolo - a fresh raviolo filled with ricotta and spinach and a whole egg yolk. I have included it in this book as a tribute to my time there, especially as it was one of the dishes that got me the job at the Italian Embassy.

I expected to leave after Ambassador Economides did, as it is custom for an Ambassador to choose his own staff, often starting with the chef. However the new (current) Ambassador, Pasquale Terracciano decided to keep me on, which I am extremely grateful for. For me, although it is a job, it is something that I love. It is a step away from the Michelin stars direction, allowing me to get back to my roots, where food is about trying to recreate that sense of comfort and home. It's a strange thing to do when you're in a professional environment that's all about etiquette, but I still very much try to generate a sense of comfort and add a personal touch

to the food I cook. The guests here expect something in particular. If you can't have proper Italian food that reminds you of home at the Italian Embassy, then where can you? I think a lot of the Italians who visit enjoy being reminded of home, and those of other nations expect to experience something authentic.

"The simpler the food is, the better, so the ingredients can't hide."

For events at the embassy we plan the menu two weeks before, though this often changes according to schedules of visitors and the Ambassador himself. The menus are primarily seasonal, and then are written according to the occasion. For instance a celebration or black tie dinner requires something different to a business lunch. We also plan wine pairing for each course.

There are rules to be followed here, and a lot of protocol. For instance the way in which you plate things can come under scrutiny and you can't choose the cutlery as there's an etiquette to that. You also need to be careful with how you cook some things; certain decorum requires you to serve guests in a specific order on some occasions with guests of honour, so you can't cook anything too pink as you always have to think about temperature. You also have to be careful of the furniture and the artwork as much of it is antique and exceptionally valuable. Even before you step into the kitchen there are so many aspects to think about including planning your courses around tight event schedules; things like arrival drinks, canapés and speeches all have to be adhered to. Working at the embassy is like no other environment I've ever worked in.

An event that stands out for me is Italian Republic Day, where we invite 500 guests for a reception every year. The menu for this event acts as a showcase for Italian producers, representing the best of our country and involving as many people as possible. On this occasion, I am always grateful to my suppliers; if it wasn't for them then the event wouldn't be a success at all. Diplomats in London from around the world attend each embassy's national day party, and though I wouldn't go so far as to call it a competition, there's a definite sense of pride in the festivities. Each year the Ambassador thanks me for the work we do for the event, and is always over the moon with the compliments he receives. Unsurprisingly, people always love the pizzettes, and you couldn't really host an Italian Republic Day party without these traditional and iconic aperitivos. Like every other big event, the tomato arancine and aubergine burgers are also big hits. Despite being so simple (and I'll admit perhaps a little overused) these are the things that people always ask for. So why turn your back on something people love? Give them a go yourself, I guarantee your friends and family will ask for them time and time again.

Sometimes we're not informed of important events or dinners until the last minute. About two years ago I received a phone call whilst I was away from the embassy – I was actually in a police station as I had lost my ID – and was told there would be a dinner that evening for Tony Blair, the Ambassador and the Italian Prime Minister Matteo Renzi. It was 3pm at the time so I really didn't have long to pull something together. Though there was some initial panic, luckily the way we work involves being prepared for occasions just like this. I prepared a smoked mackerel salad, not dissimilar to the recipe I've included in this book, and the multicolour tortellini which you'll find on page 172. I remember Tony Blair particularly enjoyed the course where we served a simple roast turbot dish, though he regretted he couldn't enjoy the wine pairings we'd chosen as he wasn't drinking due to it being the period of Lent.

The biggest part of the job is to source products. In my eyes, the simpler the food is, the better, so the ingredients can't hide. You need to start with the very best and allow them to shine. In London you can find everything you need on a daily basis from various wholesalers, markets, shops and supermarkets.

"Being on MasterChef landed me in one of the most demanding situations I've ever found myself in."

One of the reasons I entered MasterChef: The Professionals in 2015 was because I wanted to shed some light on the Italian Embassy in London and raise the profile of the work we do here. It's incredible how much people don't know. The residency at the embassy is an important job that helps everyone, creating contacts, networks and opportunities for people. In the kitchen alone I provide training, taking chefs from Italy and helping them take a further step in their career. We are a true representation of Italy and the food we serve reflects that, showing off different dishes from different regions and helping out companies and people by championing their products.

Though I was expecting it to be difficult, competing on MasterChef was one of the hardest challenges of my career. It was incredibly nerve-wracking and I constantly kept questioning myself. While you're at home watching an hour's show you only catch a few highlights, whereas in that one hour we've worked an entire shift in a kitchen we're not used to, with a style of cooking we may not have ever done before. It really is the most tense and demanding situation I've ever found myself in. However it is an experience I will always cherish; just as I left my comfort zone when I left Italy, I found myself faced with the same thing when I entered MasterChef. I was forced to be creative and resourceful. It's incredible how much I grew as a chef in such a short amount of time. Reaching the final felt like an enormous achievement.

"Working at the embassy I'm representing Italian cooking in London. It is empowering."

I have a few reasons for writing this book now. It is coming to the end of the Ambassador's term and who knows when I will have another opportunity like this to showcase not only my own cooking but Italian products, dishes and the good work that the embassy does. Working here I'm representing Italian cooking in London. It is empowering, it has made me understand what we're doing. It's great to open the door on the menu of the Italian Embassy and offer an insight into what goes on here, through the perspective of the kitchen.

The book is divided not simply into starters, mains and desserts because as Italians, we see it differently. We're not quite satisfied with just three courses and dinner is never something to be rushed; you'll find aperitivos, starters, pasta courses, main courses, salads and desserts. Take your time, enjoy the cooking process, and most importantly savour your meals with your friends and family.

For me, it felt natural to divide the book into sections based on style of occasion. The way it has been organised reflects how I plan my menus at the Italian Embassy, and certain recipes are perfect for particular events. However, each dish is applicable to home cooking; my advice is to think about who you are cooking for. If you are looking to impress someone, go for a dish from the pranzi di gala section, or if you are cooking for your family the il pranzo della Domenica chapter is made for you. Finally, nothing is regimented in this book. Have a browse and feel free to mix and interpret dishes and elements of recipes as you like. Italian food is about comfort, tradition, humble ingredients, full flavours and most of all, passion. Buon Appetito!

FOODCYCLE

This is a charity that is close to my heart. After working for so long in the industry, I have seen first-hand the amount of food that is wasted, which is a travesty considering there are so many who don't have enough to eat.

FoodCycle is a national charity that combines volunteers, surplus food and spare kitchen spaces to create tasty, nutritious meals for people at risk of food poverty and social isolation.

As it stands, they currently run 29 projects across the country. One huge part of their ethos is that eating together is one of the most important things – it's what unites us and it's one of life's simplest pleasures. For many guests, a weekly FoodCycle meal is one of the few opportunities they have to sit down and eat with someone.

The charity addresses food poverty by serving hot, nutritious three-course meals to those that would otherwise struggle to access healthy affordable food. They also work to reduce social isolation by creating chances for those affected by loneliness to socialise and feel valued as part of their community.

Their volunteers work with local retailers to use surplus food that would otherwise go to waste. In partnership with charities and community groups, these ingredients are cooked into delicious meals and served to guests. And they don't just serve any food, but good food: meals are cooked from scratch, often including five portions of fruit and vegetables.

I first started my involvement with them in early 2016 when I took part in their annual fundraising dinner. One of the prizes of the fundraising auction was a dinner cooked by me.

I am from a very humble family where nothing goes to waste; over-ripe fruit becomes marmalade, cheese crusts go into soups, old eggs become custard, and so on. Mealtimes were always a time to spend together with the people you love, so finding a charity that encompasses these same values to me was heart-warming.

We live with so many surpluses but still lots of us suffer from food poverty, and there are many people at risk of isolation, even though they may live in big cities with huge communities. The FoodCycle volunteers are modern-day heroes that fight against these plagues.

COLAZIONI DI LAVORO
Business lunches and dinners

These lunches and dinners can be quite serious occasions, and are usually hosted prior to or following an important meeting discussing business negotiations or relationships between countries. We welcome a lot of well-travelled international guests at the embassy, and they may have certain expectations of authentic Italian food, so you can't let them down.

While our guests don't come here primarily for the food, I believe it plays an important role – it's always better to make a decision on a full stomach after all!

The recipes that you'll find in this section are mostly very light and healthy, and they won't require much time to prepare.

INSALATA DI SGOMBRO AFFUMICATO, POMODORO E ANGURIA PICCANTE

smoked mackerel salad with pink bull's heart tomatoes, watermelon and chilli

SERVES: 4 | PREPARATION TIME: 50 MINUTES (PLUS TIME TO MARINATE OVERNIGHT)

The risk of contamination related to raw fish is the same for the marinated fish. This implies that we treat it in the same way, freezing it at -20°C for 24 hours, to prevent any risk of infection. Remember, marinated doesn't mean cooked. Make sure the fish has been fully defrosted.

A very fresh and summery salad, this recipe is the result of a slightly unusual pairing of ingredients. It's a prime example of how creativity in the kitchen can bare wonderful and exciting results. The rich smokiness of the mackerel goes beautifully with the mild acidity of the meaty bull's heart tomato, combined with apple cider vinegar and the sweetness of the watermelon topped with a hit of chilli. I use a slightly unconventional method to smoke fish, using aromatic woods (hazelnut wood, olive trees, dry olive leaves, rosemary). If these are not available to you, replace them with wood chips, as you would for a barbecue.

2 X 800g whole mackerel

150g salt

100g sugar

Black pepper, to taste

Handful of wood chips

2 pink bull's heart tomatoes

500g watermelon, cleaned

1 tsp powdered sweet chilli

20g roasted almonds

1 tbsp apple cider vinegar

2 tbsp extra virgin olive oil

Salt flakes and black pepper, to taste

1 small bunch of mixed fresh herbs/ leaves (e.g. pea shoots, basil, rocket leaves)

To clean the gut from the fish, you need to insert scissors into its belly and draw them towards the head. Open the belly of the fish with scissors, remove the gut and rinse the fish in cold water. After cleaning the gut from the fish, pat it dry with a kitchen towel. With a very sharp knife, remove the fillets from the bone by lifting it away from the bones and with the help of fish tweezers, remove the tiny pin bones from the fillets. Keep the fish fillets aside, leaving the skin on.

Combine the salt and the sugar with a bit of black pepper. In a container, cover the fish fillets with this salt and sugar mixture. Leave in the fridge to marinate overnight, or ideally for 24 hours. Later, rinse the fish under running water and pat dry with a tea towel.

In a small casserole dish fire up the woodchips and smoke the mackerel fillets. You can use the oven as a smoking chamber and place the fish fillets over the rack, alternatively a deep baking tray with a lid will work just as well. The fish shouldn't be in direct contact with the wood. Smoke for 15 minutes and repeat the treatment twice using the same wood to give a stronger flavour. Set aside.

Cut the tomatoes into large segments. Cut the watermelon into large cubes, removing the rind, and sprinkle with chilli powder. Roughly chop the roasted almonds.

Before plating, dress the mackerel with apple cider vinegar. Place the watermelon cubes and tomato segments on the plate. Add the mackerel and top with almond flakes. Drizzle with extra virgin olive oil, sea salt flakes and black pepper. Garnish with fresh herbs and leaves.

UOVO AGLI ASPARAGI
crispy egg with asparagus

SERVES: 4 | PREPARATION TIME: 30 MINUTES | COOKING TIME: 15 MINUTES

This is a fantastic recipe that, if cooked to perfection, delights guests with a crispy deep fried egg that still retains a runny egg yolk. Egg and asparagus is a great match and this dish is the perfect rendezvous of simplicity and technique to enhance the quality of the ingredients.

FOR ASPARAGUS SAUCE

100g shallot chopped

2 tbsp extra virgin olive oil

50g potatoes

250g green asparagus, cleaned

Salt and pepper, to taste

FOR THE HERB BREADCRUMBS

300g chopped white bread, crust removed

200g fresh herbs (basil, parsley and dill)

10g Grana Padano cheese, grated

Salt and pepper, to taste

FOR THE CRISPY EGG

4 free range eggs

Flour, to dust

1 egg, for egg wash

1 litre vegetable oil

Salt and pepper, to taste

1 small bunch of basil

To prepare the asparagus sauce, sweat the shallot in a casserole dish with a drizzle of oil and a pinch of salt. Once caramelised, slice the potatoes thinly, with a mandoline slicer if you have one, and add them to the shallot. Pour in a glass of water and cook until soft.

Trim off the woody bottom ends of the asparagus stalks. Peel with a potato peeler and boil in salted water for 1 minute. Cool down in iced water to retain the green colour. Cut off the tips and set aside to use as garnish. Chop the asparagus left and stir into the shallot. Blend the sauce until smooth and season with salt and pepper.

For the herb breadcrumbs, mix all the ingredients in a food processor until uniform in colour.

Cook the eggs for precisely 5 minutes in boiling water and cool down immediately in a bowl with iced water. Peel the eggs carefully.

Dust the egg with flour, then dip in the egg wash and roll gently in the herb breadcrumbs to coat. Coat one more time with only egg wash and breadcrumbs.

Deep fry the eggs in hot oil at 150°C for 3 minutes until golden and crispy all around. Drain on kitchen paper and add a pinch of salt.

Spread the hot asparagus sauce on the bottom of large bowls, add the asparagus tops creating a nest for the crispy egg.

Grind some fresh pepper over the top and garnish with fresh basil leaves. Serve with a drizzle of oil.

PASSATA DI CARCIOFI CON SCAMPI E BOTTARGA

artichoke veloutè with langoustines and bottarga

SERVES: 4 | PREPARATION TIME: 45 MINUTES | COOKING TIME: 30 MINUTES

In all cuisines it's very common to match bitterness with sweetness and a great example for Italians is to pair artichoke and shellfish. You'll find many recipes with artichoke and prawns or lobster and so on. This delicate passata is the perfect choice to start a light lunch meeting, or simply treat yourself with a refined dish.

This dish can be really elevated by finishing off with fresh orange zest, but if you can find *bottarga* (salted and sun-dried fish roe sacks, either mullet or tuna) then you won't regret it.

6 spiky artichokes

1 lemon squeezed

200ml white wine vinegar

Salt and pepper, to taste

1 large shallot, chopped

3 tbsp extra virgin olive oil

1 small white potato, finely cut

12 medium size langoustines

16g bottarga, freshly grated

Parsley leaves, fried

Fresh herbs, to garnish

Clean the artichokes, pull off the external hard leaves, discard the woody part and peel the stem left with a peeler. Then trim the top if too hard, cut the heart in a half and remove the "fuzzy" choke with a small paring knife.

Drop the cut artichokes straight away in cold water with lemon juice to prevent oxidation.

In a large pot bring 2 litres of water with vinegar and a pinch of salt to the boil. Cook the artichokes in the boiling water for 5 minutes. Drain and let them cool down.

In a saucepan sweat the shallot with a pinch of salt and a drizzle of oil, add the potato and a ladleful of water and let it cook for 10 minutes until soft. Add the cooked artichokes and blend until smooth. Pass through a fine sieve if needed. Season with salt and pepper to taste and keep warm.

Pull the head off the langoustines and peel them. Always keep the shell and save it for a delicious stock to be used in other dishes. Preheat a non-stick pan, de-vein the shellfish and dress it with salt and pepper. Roast the langoustines with a drizzle of olive oil on a high heat for 1 minute each side until golden.

Pour the hot artichoke passata in salad bowls, add the roast langoustines and top with fresh herbs, fried parsley leaves and abundant grated bottarga.

TONNO, FAGIOLI E CIPOLLA
tuna, onion and beans

SERVES: 4 | PREPARATION TIME: 1 HOUR 30 MINUTES (PLUS OVERNIGHT FOR SOAKING AND 6 HOURS FOR MARINATING) | COOKING TIME: 2 HOURS

The original version of this traditional dish is a salad made of tuna, beans and red Tropea onions. It tends to divide people – they either love it or hate it! It works as a summery main course but most of the time is served as a hearty starter. With borlotti bean purée, seared tuna carpaccio and pickled red onion, my interpretation makes a lovely and delicate dish of something traditionally rustic.

400g fresh tuna loin

50ml soy sauce

1 tbsp extra virgin olive oil

1 clove garlic, chopped

1 small bunch of aromatic herbs

100g cooked cannellini beans (same procedure as borlotti on page 86)

1 red chilli, chopped

80g pickled Tropea onion (see page 219)

FOR BEAN PURÉE

150g dried borlotti beans

1 pork rind (optional)

50g Grana Padano crust

1 small bunch of aromatic herbs (thyme, sage and bay laurel)

50g onion, thinly cut

25g celery, thinly cut

50g potatoes, thinly cut

50g carrot, thinly cut

1 tbsp extra virgin olive oil

Salt and pepper, to taste

50g tomato paste

Place the dried borlotti beans in cold water to soak overnight.

Put the tuna loin in the freezer for 1 hour.

Sear the cold tuna on a non-stick pan with a drizzle of oil. After a few seconds each side, the loin should be golden all around but raw and red inside. Let the fish rest and marinate it with the soy sauce, oil, garlic and herbs for about 6 hours in the fridge.

Drain the beans, then cover with cold water and bring to the boil slowly with the pork rind, the cheese crust, pinch of salt and pepper and a bouquet garnì made of aromatic herbs and keep simmering for about 1 hour and half. Meanwhile in a large casserole dish sweat the onion with celery, potatoes and carrots, a drizzle of oil and a pinch of salt.

Once the beans are well cooked take out the pork rind, the herbs and the Grana Padano crust.

Add the beans to the vegetables with all the water. Add the tomato paste, and let the soup simmer until everything is soft and well cooked.

Blend well and sieve it until smooth.

Spread the bean purée on the bottom of shallow bowls, top with cannellini beans and the tuna loin sliced at room temperature. Drizzle with extra virgin olive oil and garnish with pickled red onion, chopped chilli and fresh herbs. Season with sea salt flakes and freshly ground black pepper to taste.

SGOMBRO MARINATO CON ASPARAGI SELVATICI E MOZZARELLA DI BUFALA

mackerel with wild asparagus and buffalo mozzarella

SERVES 4 | PREPARATION TIME: 40 MINUTES | COOKING TIME: 5 MINUTES

Be careful with this recipe. Freeze the mackerel to -20°C for at least 24 hours. The risk of contamination related to raw fish is the same for marinated fish. This implies that we treat it in the same way to prevent any risk of infection. Remember – marinated doesn't mean cooked. Make sure it is thoroughly defrosted before using.

This dish is the perfect springtime starter. I really like mackerel, not only for its healthy properties but for its meaty texture too; it goes extremely well with the sweetness of the buffalo mozzarella in this dish. I usually use wild asparagus as their thin sprouts are much crunchier than the regular asparagus, and they offer earthy, woody and grassy flavours too. Of course the production time of wild vegetables is dictated by nature, so this recipe is best made in early spring until the end of April.

2 X 600g whole mackerels

200g of wild asparagus

2 vine tomatoes

Salt and pepper, to taste

1 small bunch basil

150g fresh buffalo mozzarella

3 tbsp Imperiale d'Abruzzo extra virgin olive oil

A pinch of sea salt flakes

Olive powder and breadcrumbs, to garnish (optional)

FOR THE FISH MARINADE

160ml white wine vinegar

40g table salt

80g sugar granulated

Start with the fish. To clean the fish from the gut, you need to insert scissors into its stomach and draw them towards the head. Open the stomach of the fish with scissors, remove the gut and rinse the fish in cold water. After cleaning the fish from the gut, pat it dry with a kitchen towel. With a very sharp knife, remove the fillets from the central bone by lifting it away and with the help of fish tweezers, remove the tiny pin bones left from the fillets. Keep the fish fillets aside, leaving the skin on.

To prepare the marinade, whisk the white wine vinegar with the salt and sugar in a bowl until everything is well dissolved.

Trim the asparagus by discarding the woody end part of the stalk, which you can easily do by snapping the asparagus by hand a couple of inches from the bottom. Then proceed to wash them under running water and boil them in salted water for 1 minute. Let them cool down in iced water so they retain their beautiful colour.

To peel the tomatoes, blanch them in boiling water for about 30 seconds, and let them cool down in iced water. This will allow you to easily peel the skin off the tomatoes, and chop them up roughly.

Dress the chopped tomatoes with a drizzle of extra virgin olive oil, salt and pepper and a few leaves of basil. Here, you can also add a touch of garlic if you would like to.

Cut the mozzarella into rough cubes, and put the mackerel fillets into the marinade, where they should rest for no longer than 5 minutes.

After 5 minutes, remove the fish from the marinade, and pat dry with a kitchen towel. Using a blowtorch, or under a very hot grill, burn the skin of the mackerel, and proceed to plating.

The chopped tomatoes are to be put first on the plate. I usually use a large plate for this starter. Add the mozzarella cubes, and top with the mackerel fillets, skin side up. Top it all with the wild asparagus that have been dressed in extra virgin olive oil, and for the finishing touch, sprinkle with some basil leaves and sea salt flakes.

If you want to add a little extra to the dish, you can roast some breadcrumbs and sprinkle them, as well as olive powder, on top of the fillets.

VELLUTATA DI ZUCCA CON RICOTTA DI BUFALA E NOCCIOLE

pumpkin velouté with buffalo ricotta cheese and hazelnuts

SERVES 4 | PREPARATION TIME: 20 MINUTES | COOKING TIME: 30 MINUTES

Just before I was about to try this dish for the first time, I knew I was going to like it. Do you know this feeling? Observing the ingredients, you picture them in your mouth and you think what a perfect match! Italian violin pumpkin (it looks like a violin) at its best from mid September until December, super fresh buffalo ricotta cheese and hazelnuts, a perfect triangle! Trust me the simplicity of this recipe will make you fall in love with it too. If you cannot find fresh buffalo ricotta the regular ricotta is a valid alternative.

1kg pumpkin

1 golden onion

3 tbsp extra virgin olive oil

Salt and pepper, to taste

160g fresh buffalo ricotta cheese

40g roasted hazelnuts

2 sage leaves

Black pepper

Peel the pumpkin and scrape out all the seeds. Finely chop the onion and sweat on a low heat in a casserole dish with a drizzle of oil and a pinch of salt and the sage leaves.

Add the roughly chopped pumpkin and cook on a medium heat with the lid on for at least 15 minutes. If the pumpkin gets too dry add a splash of water.

Once the pumpkin is cooked, remove the sage and then mash and blend it well until smooth, then season to taste.

Pour the hot velouté in deep bowls and scoop the fresh buffalo ricotta on top using an ice-cream scoop or a big spoon.

Chop the pre-roasted hazelnuts and coat the ricotta cheese only.

Finish with a drizzle of extra virgin olive oil and some freshly ground black pepper.

Serve immediately.

INSALATA DI PUNTARELLE CON BURRATA

puntarelle salad with burrata cheese

SERVES: 4 | PREPARATION TIME: 20 MINUTES

Puntarelle is a variant of chicory, which is usually picked when it is still very young and tender. It has an elongated shape, and the best parts are the shoots and the top, which are usually eaten raw in salads.

The outside leaf is also enjoyed cooked. It has a very bitter yet pleasant taste. Traditionally, *puntarelle* are prepared in salads. The most famous is known as *puntarelle alla Romana*, a Roman style salad. It is prepared with extra virgin olive oil, anchovies, garlic and vinegar. I love this dish, but enjoy it more paired with burrata, thanks to its sweet acidity, which complements the *puntarelle's* bitterness.

This is a very simple recipe. It can be both elegant and rustic, and as every Italian recipe that I love, it is as simple as the quality of the ingredients. Rely on good ingredients and the recipe will be successful.

1 puntarelle	Rinse the puntarelle and discard any large or tough outside leaves.
4 anchovies	Open the tops and chop thinly with a sharp knife.
3 tbsp Imperiale d'Abruzzo extra virgin olive oil	Drop the puntarelle in iced cold water and leave to rest for 30 minutes so they become crispy and curly. Drain.
Salt and pepper, to taste	Chop the anchovies roughly.
1 tsp balsamic vinegar	Create an emulsion by mixing extra virgin olive oil, anchovies, a pinch of salt and white wine vinegar together. Use this emulsion as a dressing for the puntarelle.
1 small bunch fresh herbs	
250g fresh burrata cheese	Place the puntarelle in a bowl and dress with the emulsion.
	Garnish with some fresh herbs and top the puntarelle salad with a half burrata cheese per guest.
	Add a pinch of salt, black pepper and a drizzle of extra virgin olive oil to the burrata.

PASSATA DI CECI CON GAMBERI ROSSI

chickpea soup with sicilian red prawns

SERVES: 4 | PREPARATION TIME: 45 MINUTES (PLUS OVERNIGHT TO SOAK THE CHICKPEAS) | COOKING TIME: 2 HOURS

A modern dish of traditional heritage. The rustic Tuscan chickpea soup is transformed into a smooth elegant veloutè and served with roasted red prawns. This recipe was inspired by Italian chef *Fulvio Pierangelini*.

150g dried chickpeas

1 onion

1 large carrot

1 clove garlic

Prosciutto rind (optional)

1 bay leaf

1 tbsp tomato paste

12 fresh medium Sicilian red prawns

1 small bunch of rosemary

4 tbsp extra virgin olive oil

Salt and pepper, to taste

Wash the chickpeas under running water and soak overnight. Roast the vegetables with a drizzle of oil and a pinch of salt. Simmer the chickpeas with roast onion, carrot, garlic, prosciutto rind (if using) and bay leaf. Add a drizzle of oil, season with salt and pepper and cook for about 1½ hours. Do not use too much water only the quantity needed to cover the chickpeas.

Remove everything from the cooking stock and set aside. Peel some whole chickpeas and leave them in the cooking stock to use as a garnish later.

Discard the rind, garlic and bay leaf. Blend the chickpeas with the tomato paste, onion and carrot, adding cooking water until smooth but thick. Pass the soup through a fine sieve if necessary.

Clean the prawns, peel and de-vein. Quickly pan-roast them with extra virgin olive oil, salt and pepper.

Pour the hot chickpea soup in bowls, garnish with skinned whole chickpeas and top with roasted prawns. Drizzle over extra virgin olive oil and freshly chopped rosemary.

BACCALÀ MANTECATO CON MAIS CORVINO

creamy salted cod with corn corvino polenta

SERVES: 4 | PREPARATION TIME: 30 MINUTES | COOKING TIME: 40 MINUTES

Baccalà is traditional Italian salted cod; an ingredient that has recently become more popular in the UK. As it is salted, you need to make sure to rehydrate it in running water before use. This preparation is most famously known as *baccalà mantecato alla Veneziana*, as it is typical around Venice. Blended *baccalà* with a touch of cream, milk and plenty of extra virgin olive oil gives it the appearance of a fish mousse. It is usually served with creamy polenta, however, I use a special type of corn, an ancient dark corn called corvino. This wonderful product has a black pigment which is extremely rich in beta carotene, is very rich in natural antioxidants and is gluten-free. Not only is *mais corvino* healthy, it also has a deeper and richer flavour than a regular corn polenta.

FOR THE BACCALÀ MANTECATO

250g steamed baccalà

50ml milk

50ml double cream

Salt and pepper, to taste

300ml extra virgin olive oil

FOR THE MAIS CORVINO POLENTA

1 litre water

Salt and pepper, to taste

250g mais corvino

Stale bread

20g pickled red onion (see page 219)

1 small bunch of fresh herbs (e.g. dill, chives and basil)

1 tsp extra virgin olive oil

Start with the baccalà. Put it in a food processor with the milk and cream. Blend for about 30 seconds and season with salt and pepper. Blend again while gradually pouring in the extra virgin olive oil. The mixture should become thicker and creamier. Set aside and store it in the fridge.

For the mais corvino polenta, bring the water to boiling point with a drizzle of extra virgin olive oil and a pinch of salt and pepper. Add the corn corvino gradually to avoid getting lumps and cook on a low heat for approximately 40 minutes. Keep stirring once in a while. When ready, set aside.

Chop the stale bread and roast as garnish. Now proceed to plating. Place a couple of spoonfuls of the creamy mais corvino on the plate, top with baccalà mantecato and crispy bread. Garnish with the pickled red onion and fresh herbs. Drizzle with extra virgin olive oil. Serve the corn warm and baccalà at room temperature.

LINGUINE CON CICALE DI MARE E ZUCCHINE

linguine with mantis shrimp and courgette

SERVES: 4 | PREPARATION TIME: 25 MINUTES | COOKING TIME: 30 MINUTES

Mantis shrimp is the translation for this lovely shellfish but I bet not many people have heard of it in the UK! It is very common in the Mediterranean area, and goes by a number of names depending upon where you are in Italy... *canocchie, pannocchie, cicale, sparnocchia* and so on! I don't mind what you call it, I just hope you adore this fish as much as I do.

With incredibly sweet, delicate and soft meat, they can be a pain to clean but once the job is done the cicale makes the perfect shellfish for a beautiful plate of seafood pasta or a great *guazzetto* (stew). Traditionally it is cooked in the shell, but I prefer to use the shell for fish stocks and the lovely meat as sauce for linguine condiment.

Great pasta from *Gragnano* producer *Caccese*, sweet *cicale di mare*, courgette with flowers and as a final touch a hint of salty bottarga; this plate of linguine will turn your day around!

700g cicale di mare

1 onion, chopped

100ml dry white wine

3 green courgettes, with flowers

320g linguine di Gragnano Caccese

3 tbsp extra virgin olive oil

1 clove garlic, chopped

½ chilli, chopped

Salt and pepper, to taste

1 small bunch of fresh herbs (basil, parsley)

10g grated tuna (bottarga)

Start by peeling the cicale di mare with sharp scissors. Cut the heads off and trim the body all around the edges. This procedure will help you to gently discard the upper part of the shell and remove the meat from the crustaceous safely. Remember to save all liquids and trimmings for the stock.

Sweat the onion in a large casserole dish with a pinch of salt and a drizzle of olive oil. Once golden add all the shellfish trimmings and cook for about 3 minutes. Season with salt and pepper and pour in the white wine. Allow the alcohol to evaporate and cover the trimmings with cold water. Simmer for 5 minutes and pass it through a fine sieve. Keep the stock aside.

Remove the flowers from the courgettes, get rid of the pistils, wash quickly and cut roughly. Rinse the courgettes thoroughly and slice very thinly.

Drop the pasta in salted boiling water, stir and cook for about 8 minutes until al dente. Meanwhile prepare the condiment. Gently heat a couple of tablespoons of olive oil in a large pan, add the garlic and chilli and cook for a couple of minutes. Add the courgettes with flowers and keep cooking for 1 more minute. Add 1 ladleful of shellfish stock to the condiment and drain the linguine al dente into the sauce. Now is time to drop the cicale into the pasta, add an extra drizzle of oil and stir and toss on high heat for 30 seconds until creamy.

Season to taste and plate straight away. Garnish the linguine with fresh herbs and top with grated bottarga.

PACCHERI ALLE VONGOLE VERACI CON ROMANESCO E BOTTARGA

paccheri with fresh clams, romanesco cauliflower and bottarga

SERVES 4 | PREPARATION TIME: 40 MINUTES (PLUS 2 HOURS TO SOAK THE CLAMS) | COOKING TIME: 20 MINUTES

This plate of pasta is perfect for a summer lunch. *Paccheri* is a large shaped pasta, very traditional in the south of Italy, and goes perfectly with any kind of shellfish. Romanesco cauliflower isn't largely common in the UK, yet it is extremely tasty with rich earthy flavour and pairs beautifully with fresh clams. I use *bottarga* to complement this dish. *Bottarga* are salted fish roe from tuna or mullet, very traditional in Sardinia.

500g fresh clams

300g dried Gragnano paccheri pasta Caccese

3 tbsp Imperiale d'Abruzzo extra virgin olive oil

2 garlic cloves

2 parsley stalks

1 red chilli

100ml dry white wine

1 romanesco cauliflower

20g white onion

Salt and pepper, to taste

Parsley, to garnish

30g tuna bottarga

Place the clams in a large bowl, cover with cold water and a pinch of salt. Leave to sit for a couple of hours, allowing any sediment to remove itself from the shells.

Drop the pasta into salted boiling water; usually this shape of pasta takes around 15 minutes to cook.

Rinse the clams thoroughly and scrub them in cold water. Discard any cracked, damaged or open shells. To cook the clams, drizzle extra virgin olive oil in a pan, add garlic, a couple of parsley stalks and half of the red chilli. Once it is well heated, add the clams, pour the white wine in, cover and let it cook for 3-4 minutes until all the clams are open. Remove garlic, chilli, parsley stalk and any clams that do not open during the cooking process, as they might contain sand. Meanwhile, trim and clean the cauliflower from its leaves. Cut the cauliflower into individual florets from the central stem with the help of a paring knife. Boil the florets in salted water for about 3-4 minutes, depending on size. Cool in iced water to retain colour. You could also make a cauliflower purée with the leftover trimmings, by simply boiling and blending them with a bit of water.

Sauté the onion on the side, with a bit of chopped garlic and the leftover red chilli, chopped. Add the cauliflower florets and once slightly roasted, add the clams with all of the fragrant cooking juice.

Make sure to cook the pasta until al dente – slightly firm to the bite. Add the cooked pasta to the pan with the clams and cauliflower. Keep stirring for 1 minute.

Once the sauce has started to reduce, add a drizzle of extra virgin olive oil and toss the pan for a little longer, to create a flavoursome emulsion.

Remember that clams are naturally salty so taste and add salt and pepper to your liking.

For the garnish, you can either remove some clams from their shell or leave them as they are. Plate the hot pasta in large pasta bowls. Garnish with parsley and sprinkle the bowl with grated bottarga.

SPAGHETTI CON ACCIUGHE E FINOCCHIO

spaghetti with anchovies and fennel

SERVES: 4 | PREPARATION TIME: 30 MINUTES | COOKING TIME: 30 MINUTES

A Sicilian inspired pasta dish full of character and flavour. I personally love the balance between the mild sulphur note of wild fennel and the savouriness of anchovies. Combined together with zesty orange, this makes for a lively plate of spaghetti.

50g onion, chopped

2 tbsp extra virgin olive oil

I bulb fennel, finely chopped

50g anchovies

I clove garlic, chopped

20g unsalted butter

100ml prosecco DOC

320g Gragnano spaghetti Caccese

I orange, zest

I small bunch wild fennel (or dill)

Salt and pepper, to taste

Sweat the onion in a large casserole dish with a drizzle of oil and a pinch of salt. Once golden add the finely chopped fennel and keep cooking on a low heat for about 8 minutes until the fennel becomes soft. Blend well, pass through a fine sieve and season to taste. Keep the fennel purée aside.

Drain the anchovy fillets and cut them into strips.

In a large pan fry the garlic with a knob of butter and once golden pour in the prosecco and let the alcohol evaporate. Add the fennel purée.

Cook the pasta in salted boiling water until al dente and drain it into the pan with the fennel purée. Stir and toss the spaghetti well, add a drizzle of extra virgin olive oil and a couple of ladles of cooking water. Keep stirring for I minute until the spaghetti becomes creamy. Toss in the anchovies and plate straight away.

Garnish the spaghetti with fresh wild fennel leaves and orange zest.

TRIGLIA FARCITA, CAPONATA E SALSA DI MOZZARELLA DI BUFALA AFFUMICATA

stuffed red mullet with caponata & smoked buffalo mozzarella sauce

SERVES: 4 | PREPARATION TIME: 1 HOUR 15 MINUTES | COOKING TIME: 20 MINUTES

In Italy, red mullet is usually quite a small fish, and the smaller the fish, the richer the flavour is. It does however require longer to be cleaned and pin boned. It goes beautifully with the sweetness of Sicilian red prawns and the freshness of summer vegetables. With everything paired with a rich smoky buffalo mozzarella sauce, you've set yourself up for a heavenly treat.

4 X 300g red mullet

150g Sicilian red prawns, peeled and gutted

100ml double cream

Salt and pepper, to taste

250g smoked buffalo mozzarella

2 tbsp homemade breadcrumbs

4 tbsp extra virgin olive oil

1 bulb garlic, chopped

1 lemon zest

10 cherry tomatoes

1 green courgette

1 red pepper

1 yellow pepper

1 black aubergine

4 courgette flowers

1 small bunch of fresh basil

Start by filleting the fish. Remove the guts and chop the head off. With the help of a flexible knife, fillet the fish, leaving the tail attached to both ends of the fillet. With a fish tong, remove any bones from the fillets. Keep the trimmings of the fillet, to use later for the filling. Set the fillets aside.

To prepare the filling blend the prawns and the fish trimmings with 50ml of double cream and a pinch of salt and black pepper. Blend filling in a food processor until smooth. Season the red mullets and stuff them with the filling between the two fillets for each fish, keeping a fish-like shape.

Chop the mozzarella roughly, place in bowl with the remaining double cream and let it cook slowly in a bain-marie (heatproof bowl over hot water). Do not bring to the boil, but allow to melt on a gentle heat. This will prevent the mozzarella from splitting. To prepare the crunchy breadcrumbs, roast them in a pan with a drizzle of extra virgin olive oil, chopped garlic, salt and pepper. You may add lemon zest and fresh chopped herbs.

For the caponata, blanch the cherry tomatoes in boiling water for 30 seconds, and cool down in iced water to remove the skin. Cut the courgette and peppers into small cubes. Stir fry with a drizzle of extra virgin olive oil and a pinch of salt. Repeat this for the peeled cherry tomatoes.

Chop the aubergine roughly, add salt and pepper. Roast in a frying pan with extra virgin olive oil. Once cooked, chop into a paste to create a purée.

Gently wash and open the courgette flower, and stuff with the vegetables and aubergine purée. Place it on a baking tray lined with baking parchment and bake at 180°C for 1 minute with a drizzle of extra virgin olive oil. Bake the red mullet with a drizzle of extra virgin olive oil at 180°C for 5-6 minutes. To check they're cooked, the filling should become firm.

Pass the buffalo mozzarella sauce through a fine sieve, into a saucer. Place the red mullet on the plate with the stuffed courgette flower on the side. Sprinkle roasted breadcrumbs on top of the fish and the fresh basil on top of the vegetables. Drizzle with extra virgin olive oil.

Pour a spoonful of hot smoked buffalo mozzarella sauce onto the dish before serving.

CEFALO ARROSTO IN GUAZZETTO DI CECI E VONGOLE CON SALSA VERDE

roasted grey mullet with chickpea and clam guazzetto and salsa verde

SERVES: 4 | PREPARATION TIME: 1 HOUR (PLUS OVERNIGHT TO SOAK THE CHICKPEAS) | COOKING TIME: 1½ HOURS

Grey mullet is a lovely fish, often underestimated, it can be confused with sea bass for its white meat but mullets have a broad flat head and larger scales. Never overcook fish otherwise it becomes dry and tough. The salty clam and chickpea *guazzetto* works beautifully with the mild aromatic tanginess of homemade salsa verde.

500g dried chickpeas

Salt and pepper, to taste

3 tbsp extra virgin olive oil

1 bunch mixed fresh herbs (thyme, bay leaf and rosemary)

1 large onion

2 carrots

1 celery stalk

2 bulbs garlic

1 red chilli

Small bunch parsley

10ml prosecco DOC

500g fresh clams

4 X 250g grey mullet fillets, pin boned

4 tbsp salsa verde, (see page 216)

Soak the chickpeas in cold water overnight.

Simmer the chickpeas with a pinch of salt, black pepper, a drizzle of olive oil, herbs and the trimmed vegetables. Once cooked let the chickpeas cool down in their own water. Discard the herbs and vegetables.

Blend some of the chickpeas with a bit of cooking water to obtain a purée to be used as base for the fish fillets and keep warm.

Purge and remove the sand from the clams, rinse them well and preheat a saucepan. Cook the clams on high heat with a drizzle of oil, 1 garlic bulb, chilli and parsley and cover the pan. After 2 minutes pour in the prosecco and keep cooking until the clams are fully opened.

Discard the shell from the clams and put them back in the sieved seafood juice.

In a casserole dish add the chickpeas to the clams and add both of the cooking water to get a very tasty guazzetto. Do not add any extra salt as clams are already salty. Add some chopped fresh parsley and keep warm.

Meanwhile dress the mullets with salt and pepper and roast them on high heat in a non-stick pan with a drizzle of oil. Once both sides are golden remove from the heat and move to plating.

Pour the guazzetto on the bottom of large bowls, add a spoon of chickpea purée and place the mullets on top of it. Garnish the dish with a nice spoon of fresh homemade salsa verde.

SGROPPINO AL LIMONE E PROSECCO DOC

lemon sgroppino with prosecco

SERVES: 6 | PREPARATION TIME: 10 MINUTES | COOKING TIME: 5 MINUTES

This is a classic Venetian recipe of lemon sorbet and prosecco. The wonderful region of *Veneto* is not just the birthplace of this recipe but perhaps more importantly, the home of prosecco, an incredible versatile wine.

Sgroppino isn't quite a dessert, but more of a palate cleanser, to be served in between courses. It has actually become so popular over time that it's often enjoyed as a refreshing cocktail.

Personally I love the combination between the beautiful flavour of unwaxed *Amalfi* lemon, an excellent prosecco DOC and a hint of mint. Fresh and dairy-free, this is a real treat.

250g sugar

500ml water

1 unwaxed Amalfi lemon

250ml prosecco DOC

Fresh mint, to garnish

Start by making the lemon sorbet.

In a saucepan, combine the sugar and water.

Add the grated lemon zest to the saucepan, then cut the lemon in half and add the juice to the saucepan.

Bring to the boil until the sugar has dissolved.

Remove from heat and allow to cool down.

Once cool, pour the syrup into the ice cream maker.

After approximately 30 minutes, when it is nice and creamy, let it set in the freezer for a couple of hours.

Put the lemon sorbet into a powerful blender, and add the prosecco.

Mix well and serve cool straight away before it loses its nice creamy consistency.

Garnish with fresh mint.

SORBETTI TRICOLORE
tricolour sorbet with strawberry, pear and basil

SERVES: 8 | PREPARATION TIME: 30 MINUTES (PLUS OF COUPLE OF HOURS TO SET) | COOKING TIME: 10 MINUTES

The main reason I serve this tricolour sorbet is for my work at the Italian Embassy but I cannot deny how good and appreciated this dish is; it is always nice to see one's flag served as dessert. After a summer meal, regardless of how filling it may have been, who can decline a sorbet to finish? Fruity, refreshing and creamy, sorbet is a guilt-free and delicious dessert.

FOR THE BASIL SORBET

500ml water

250g sugar

1 drop lemon juice

1 small bunch of basil (roughly 30g)

FOR THE STRAWBERRY SORBET

220g ripe strawberries

500ml water

200g sugar

FOR THE PEAR SORBET

400g ripe white pears

400ml water

100g sugar

30ml glucose syrup

1 drop lemon juice

Start with the basil sorbet. In a saucepan, combine water with the sugar and a drop of lemon juice. Bring to boil and let it cool down until at room temperature. Add the basil leaves to the liquid and put into a blender. Blend well and pass through a fine sieve to remove excess. Put into the ice cream maker. Once ready, after approximately 30 minutes, set aside in the freezer for a couple of hours.

For the strawberry sorbet, clean the strawberries thoroughly. Prepare the syrup by combining the water and sugar in a saucepan. Bring to boiling point. Remove from the heat and allow to cool down. Blend with the ripe strawberries, pass through a fine sieve and put into the ice cream maker. Once ready, after approximately 30 minutes, set aside in the freezer for a couple of hours.

For the pear sorbet, proceed to clean the pears. Discard the seeds and chop the pears roughly. In a saucepan, combine the water, sugar and glucose with a drop of lemon juice. Bring to boiling point. Add the white pears to the saucepan, and remove from heat. Allow the pears to cool down in the syrup. Put in a blender and blend until smooth. Put into the ice cream maker, and after approximately 30 minutes, let it set in the freezer for a couple of hours.

Plate in cold shallow bowls and serve a generous spoon of each sorbet and garnish with fresh basil or fruits.

BAVARESE AL COCCO CON CREMOSO AL CIOCCOLATO

coconut bavarois with chocolate ganache

SERVES: 4 | PREPARATION TIME: 1 HOUR 30 MINUTES (PLUS TIME FOR SETTING) | COOKING TIME: 20 MINUTES

Coconut is a tropical fruit which apparently has no Italian links, but for any Italian growing up in a seaside town like me, thanks to crafty peddlers one learns to deeply love coconut. This is an easy yet indulgent recipe, pairing chocolate and coconut; a perfect marriage for those with a sweet tooth.

FOR THE COCOA CRUMBLE

125g flour

80g unsalted butter, softened

40g caster sugar

25g cocoa powder

FOR THE CHOCOLATE GANACHE

80g egg yolk

35g sugar

150ml double cream

100ml milk

150g dark chocolate 55%

FOR THE COCONUT BAVAROIS

250ml coconut milk

60g sugar

250ml double cream

8g edible gelatine leaf (soaked)

TO GARNISH

10g roasted hazelnuts

Start with the cocoa crumble, as the base for the dessert. Make sure the butter is at room temperature. Cut roughly. Mix all the ingredients together until smooth. Wrap in cling film and leave to rest for 30 minutes. Preheat the oven to 180°C. With a rolling pin, roll out the crumble to form a 2cm thick sheet. Bake for 12 minutes. Once ready, allow it to cool down. Break the crumble into rough pieces. Set aside.

For the chocolate ganache, beat the egg yolk with the sugar until foamy. In a saucepan, heat the cream and milk gently. Pour the hot mixture onto the egg yolk and sugar. Whisk well, and bring the mixture to 80°C. Break the chocolate into rough pieces. Once it has reached the correct temperature, pour the hot mixture onto the chocolate. Mix well until the it is smooth. Set aside to cool. Once cool, pour the mixture into a pastry bag.

For the coconut bavarois, heat the coconut milk with sugar gently. Whip the cream lightly and set aside. Once the sugar has melted into the coconut milk, remove from the heat and drop the pre-soaked gelatine inside to dissolve. Set aside and allow it to cool. Fold in the whipped cream carefully. In a cake tray or portion mould, create ½cm base with the cocoa crumble (save some for the garnish), then spread the coconut bavarois mixture evenly into the mould. Allow to set in the fridge for a couple of hours.

Remove from fridge and cut into rings or slices.

Put the bavarois in the centre of the plate. Top with chocolate ganache, roasted hazelnuts and garnish with extra cocoa crumble.

PANNA COTTA ALLA VANIGLIA CON TORTA CAPRESE, FRAGOLE E BASILICO

vanilla panna cotta with caprese cake, strawberries and basil

SERVES: 4 | PREPARATION TIME: 2 HOURS | COOKING TIME: 40 MINUTES

The success of this dish lies in its very own simplicity. I only make this recipe when the ingredients are at their best in season. When trying this recipe, chef Monica Galleti said: "Wonderful, wonderful, wonderful," and remained in silence as she continued to eat it all – the highest praise you can get!

½ a caprese cake, (see page 168)

FOR THE VANILLA PANNA COTTA

375ml double cream

125ml whole milk

50g sugar

½ vanilla pod, seeds only

6g edible gelatine leaf, soaked

FOR THE COULIS AND GARNISH

300g fresh strawberries

50g sugar

100ml whipped cream

1 small bunch of fresh basil

To make the panna cotta, mix the double cream with milk, sugar and vanilla pod seeds. In a saucepan, bring the mixture to a boiling point, until the sugar is well dissolved. Remove from heat. Pour mixture in a separate bowl. Melt the pre-soaked gelatine into the panna cotta mixture, and let it cool down. Using silicone moulds, prepare 8 individual panna cottas.

Rinse the fresh strawberries in cold water. Trim the stems and cut a few strawberries into quarters to be used as a garnish. Chop the remaining strawberries and put into a casserole dish with the sugar. Let it cook gently for around 10 minutes. Blend the cooked strawberries to create a strawberry coulis, and pass through a fine sieve to remove unwanted seeds. Whip the cream and add a spoon of strawberry coulis into it and mix well.

After a couple of hours, remove the panna cotta from the fridge for plating.

Break the caprese cake into pieces and decorate the plate with them alongside a few dots of strawberry coulis and strawberry cream. With the help of a paring knife or flat knife, remove the panna cotta from its mould. Hot water may facilitate the panna cotta to be removed from its mould without damaging. Drop the panna cotta gently onto the plate. The panna cotta should be wobbly, as it is a very delicate dessert. Garnish the plate with a few leaves of fresh basil.

Though this chapter refers to Sunday lunches, you can of course enjoy these meals any day of the week. The title is more a nod to my background, and the fact that my family always gathered together on a Sunday. It would involve everyone from grandparents to cousins and most Italian families will have this tradition of regularly sharing a good quality meal with their nearest and dearest.

You'll find genuine and often quite rustic dishes from both my region of Abruzzo and the Ambassador's favourite family dishes from Naples.

IL PRANZO DELLA DOMENICA
Sunday family lunches

This section is more informal and relaxed, though the guests are no less important. For these occasions at the embassy there are often children, so you have to keep that in mind when planning a meal. For those lunches I usually try to recall something that I had during my childhood, and try to focus on something nostalgic and comforting. It can be tiring to be always following etiquette so it's nice to ease out a bit.

It does not mean that the dishes are simple – in fact many of them require a lot of time when you're making things like fresh pasta and homemade cake; there's a different kind of care that goes into it.

It's a time when I can make use of old recipes from my grandmother or mother – I have to admit, these are some of my favourites. Although I am a chef and sometimes I like to show off, I do love cooking what makes me feel better, and this food is the epitome of that.

CARCIOFINI SOTT'OLIO
pickled baby artichokes

MAKES: 4 JARS | PREPARATION TIME: 40 MINUTES | COOKING TIME: 15 MINUTES

The perfect season for baby artichokes is from March to May. I love pickling them as they're always handy in a salad or are simply delicious on crispy bruschetta.

If you make more than you need you can keep them in a dry store for up to one month.

They are usually boiled in water and vinegar and conserved in a jar with olive oil but I personally like to grill them after pickling to enrich with herbs and spices. Make sure you don't throw away the tasty oil after using them, extra virgin olive oil is like gold, don't waste it – plus, this recipe will leave you with a fantastic dressing!

30 baby artichokes

1 lemon, juice

600ml white wine vinegar

1 small bunch picked parsley, chopped

1 red chilli, chopped

4 garlic bulbs

8 black olives (optional)

1 litre Imperiale d'Abruzzo extra virgin olive oil

Salt and pepper, to taste

Clean the artichokes and pull off the external hard leaves. Discard the woody part and peel the stem left with a peeler. Then trim the top if it is too hard and cut the heart in a half. Remove the "fuzzy" choke with a small paring knife.

Drop the cut artichokes immediately into cold water with the lemon juice to prevent them from discolouring.

In a large pot bring 2 litres of water with the vinegar and a pinch of salt to the boil. Cook the artichokes in boiling water for 5 minutes. Drain, cool down and season with a drizzle of oil. Grill the artichokes (preferably on a barbecue) for 2 minutes per side.

Once cold again, put them in sterilised jars and add the parsley, chilli, garlic and olives (optional). Fill each jar with extra virgin olive oil and close tightly. Let it rest in a cool dry place for a week before enjoying them.

PALLOTTE CACIO E OVA
bread and cheese balls

SERVES: 4 | PREPARATION TIME: 30 MINUTES | COOKING TIME: 15 MINUTES

This is a traditional recipe from my beloved home region of *Abruzzo*. It is a perfect example of what we used to call *cucina povera*, (the cooking of the poor.) Originally it was made with stale bread and leftover cheese. It shows how Italians made use of humble leftovers and turned them into tasty dishes. Today we use either white, brown or sourdough bread. *Pallotte cacio e ova* was initially created as a vegetarian main course, when meat was scarce. Nowadays, it is most likely served as starter.

200g bread, crust removed

I small bunch of fresh parsley

I clove garlic, chopped

4 eggs

300g pecorino cheese, grated

I red pepper

200g tomato sauce, (see page 219)

I litre vegetable oil, for frying

I small bunch of fresh basil

2 tbsp extra virgin olive oil

100ml milk (optional)

Salt and pepper, to taste

Roughly chop the bread into small cubes. If the bread is too dry, soak it in milk first, and squeeze the excess liquid before creating the balls.

Mix the chopped bread with chopped parsley, garlic, eggs and pecorino cheese. Do not add too much salt, as pecorino cheese is already salty. Mix and knead well by hands until smooth. Create small balls. Traditionally, they should not be larger than 3cm.

As an accompaniment, chop the pepper, roast with oil and a pinch of salt and add it to the tomato sauce. Heat the vegetable oil, ready to fry the cheese balls. The balls should be fried for 2-3 minutes until golden, at a temperature of 160°C. Drain the balls from the oil, and dry on kitchen paper.

Spread a generous spoonful of tomato sauce with pepper on the centre of the plate. Gently place the cheese balls on the top. Garnish with extra cheese if desired and a few fresh basil leaves. Drizzle extra virgin olive oil on the top and serve.

PASSATA DI FAVE E FINOCCHIETTO
fennel and broad bean velvet soup

SERVES 4 | PREPARATION TIME: 20 MINUTES | COOKING TIME: 25 MINUTES

This dish is a celebration of an old Sicilian recipe. In the past people used to dry broad beans during the summer and store them for the hard winter months. Nowadays this traditional rustic recipe is more of a delicate velvet soup incorporating dill, fresh broad beans and wild fennel to create a colourful dish that still keeps the same old traditional taste.

1kg fresh broad beans

1 onion

2 whole fennel bulbs

Salt and black pepper, to taste

1 small bunch wild fennel

1 small bunch fresh herbs (including dill)

4 tbsp Imperiale d'Abruzzo extra virgin olive oil

Slit the pods along the seam and run your thumb along the furry inside to push the beans out. Cook the beans in a pot with salted boiling water for 2 minutes, drain and put them into cold iced water to retain the colour, then peel them from the thin skin around them.

Stew the onion in a saucepan with a drizzle of oil and a pinch of salt.

Cut the fennel into thin slices, cut off the hard parts (top and bottom) and add to the pan. Cover and cook for 10 minutes.

Add the broad beans (reserve some to garnish the dish) and cook for a further 5 minutes.

Blend with a mixer and add some water to adjust the density. Strain with a sieve until smooth and uniform.

Reheat quickly and season with salt and pepper to taste.

Pour the soup in bowls, add the remaining broad beans and garnish with a drizzle of extra virgin olive oil, some tops of wild fennel and fresh herbs.

GIADINIERA DI VERDURE
pickled vegetables

SERVES: 6 | PREPARATION TIME: 40 MINUTES | COOKING TIME: 20 MINUTES

Almost all of Italy boasts the tradition of pickling vegetables. It started as means of preserving vegetables, nowadays it is used mostly as antipasti, for a table to share. The word *giardiniera* means from the garden, whereby all kinds of vegetables would be pickled to be used in and out of season. They can be preserved with pickling liquid in jars for months on end.

My recipe follows a more traditional *giadiniera*, but it can be made with any seasonal vegetables.

2 carrots

2 small cucumbers

1 small bunch of red radish

4 baby artichokes

2 small bulbs fennel

Black and green olives

1 red chilli

1 tbsp extra virgin olive oil

1 small bunch of fresh herbs

2 celery stalks

Rocket, to garnish

FOR THE PICKLING LIQUID

1 litre water

1 litre white wine vinegar

40g sugar

30g salt

Wash all the vegetables thoroughly. Peel the carrots and cut into segments. Slice the cucumber in half and cut lengthways, removing the seeds. Trim the red radishes and leave them whole. Clean the artichokes and cut in half. Cut the top off the fennel and slice roughly. Peel and cut the celery.

Keep variety in the shapes of all the different vegetables.

To prepare the liquid mix all the ingredients and bring to boiling point.

Cook each vegetable separately in the pickling liquid, respecting the individual cooking time.

Cook the lighter coloured vegetables first, in order to avoid colouring the water with the darker ones.

Begin cooking the artichoke, followed by the celery, the fennel for 3 minutes, the cucumber for 2 minutes and the carrots for around 4 minutes, etc.

Once all the vegetables have been cooked al dente, strain them and discard the cooking liquid. Allow to cool.

Mix the vegetables with olives and chopped chilli. Dress with extra virgin olive oil and fresh herbs. Serve with rocket leaves.

Preserve with clean pickling liquid if you are not serving straight away.

PANZANELLA CON CALAMARI ARROSTO

tuscan panzanella with roast squid

SERVES: 4 | PREPARATION TIME: 30 MINUTES | COOKING TIME: 20 MINUTES

This simple traditional dish is another great example of *cucina povera* (the cooking of the poor). Stale bread is the main ingredient in this recipe, traditionally mixed with whatever the farmer would have at their disposal from the garden. For example, the classic *panzanella* might have been put together with fresh onions, tomatoes, peppers, herbs and dressed with extra virgin olive oil and vinegar to soften the bread. Over time, this traditional recipe is no longer just a means of using stale bread, but has grown in popularity as a refreshing starter. I particularly love serving *panzanella* with seafood, such as pan-fried squid.

500g fresh squid

400g Tuscan bread (or sourdough)

50ml white wine vinegar

3 tbsp extra virgin olive oil

Salt and pepper, to taste

1 red pepper

2 ripe plum tomatoes

½ sweet chilli

½ Tropea red onion

1 clove garlic (optional)

1 small bunch of fresh herbs, e.g. basil, parsley, dill or chives

Sea salt flakes, to garnish

When choosing the squid, opt for the smaller ones, as they are more tender and quicker to cook. Ask the fishmonger to clean the squid. If not, start by removing the mouth from the tentacles. Under the running water, remove the skin of the squid and carefully open it with a pair of sharp kitchen scissors. Clean from the inside, carefully remove the gut and the ink sac. Once clean, rinse and pat dry with a kitchen towel. Cut the squid into strips. Leave the heads as they are. Remove the crust from the bread and cut into cubes.

Soak the cubes in vinegar and dress with a drizzle of olive oil, salt and pepper to taste. Meanwhile, place the pepper on a baking tray and bake whole in the oven at 250°C for 10-15 minutes until the outside appears burnt. Remove from the oven, and place the pepper into kitchen zip bags and seal. Once cool, open the bags and rinse the peppers under running water. The skin should come off with ease. Remove the seeds from the centre of the pepper and cut it into strips. Set aside.

Blanch the tomatoes in boiling water and cool them in iced water. Peel the skin off the tomatoes and cut into rough cubes. Add the tomatoes and the pepper to the bread.

Chop the chilli and cut the onion thinly. Add these to the bread.

Dress the bread once again with a drizzle of olive oil and let it rest for 30 minutes. You can add a chopped clove of garlic at this point if you would like.

Put the panzanella in the centre of the plate and garnish with fresh herbs. Proceed to cook the squid. Heat a non-stick frying pan with a drizzle of extra virgin olive oil.

Toss the squid inside and roast for about 2 minutes until golden. Dress with salt and pepper. Top the panzanella with the roasted squid. Drizzle with extra virgin olive oil and sea salt flakes.

RADICCHIO TARDIVO ALLA GRIGLIA
barbecue tardivo radicchio

SERVES 4 | PREPARATION TIME: 30 MINUTES | COOKING TIME: 10 MINUTES

This kind of radicchio is very different from usual varieties. From the city of *Treviso*, it is called *tardivo* because it is harvested late in the season after the first frost. It is not as pink and grows into a uniquely shaped plant with elongated leaves and pronounced white cores, tinged with red. Less bitter but rich in taste, this radicchio can be expensive in price because of its long production process, but believe me it is absolutely delicious and completely worth it.

100ml balsamic vinegar

100ml extra virgin olive oil

15g sugar

4g crushed garlic

Salt and black pepper, to taste

2 radicchio tardivo di Treviso

1 small bunch chives and parsley

1 red chilli, chopped

For the marinade, whisk the balsamic vinegar, oil, sugar and garlic together in a bowl with a pinch of salt and pepper.

Wash the radicchio under cold running water and shake off any excess left in between the leaves.

When dry, cut each head of radicchio in half lengthways and brush them liberally with marinade. Leave aside for 20 minutes to marinate.

Arrange the radicchio halves cut side down on a preheat barbecue and cook for 5 minutes on each side until the stalks have tenderised slightly (you still want a bit of crunchiness!)

Put them on side plates and sprinkle with chopped herbs and a bit of fresh chilli.

Don't forget a final drizzle of extra virgin olive oil to finish the dish off.

PASSATELLI ROMAGNOLI
passatelli romagnoli

SERVES: 4 | PREPARATION TIME: 40 MINUTES | COOKING TIME: 5 MINUTES

This is a very traditional dish from *Emilia-Romagna*, with humble ingredients that are full of flavour. Delicious pasta-like dough made by breadcrumbs, *Grana Padano* cheese and eggs, shaped into a sort of thick spaghetti with a peculiar hand operated machine called a *ferro per passatelli*, which is like a potato masher or ricer. Traditionally, it is served with a rich meat broth, but there are also versions with mortadella and bone marrow.

120g homemade breadcrumbs

120g Grana Padano, grated

3 eggs

Salt and pepper, to taste

2g nutmeg, grated

1 litre beef and chicken broth

Mix the breadcrumbs with Grana Padano and drop in the eggs.

Season with salt and pepper to taste and add a little grated nutmeg.

Knead all of the ingredients together well, until you have a soft dough-like consistency. The mixture should be like a wet dough, but hard enough to hold everything together. If it seems too stiff, add 1 tablespoon of water or stock. If it's too soft, add more breadcrumbs.

Wrap the dough with cling film to retain the moisture and let it rest for 30 minutes.

Once ready, put the dough into a food mill or potato ricer with large holes. Press to create short and thick spaghetti about 4cm long.

Gently lay them over a tea towel or on a baking tray dusted with breadcrumbs.

You can either cook the passetelli in hot boiling water or straight away in the broth, but remember the cooking of it will make the broth cloudy.

Once the passatelli have risen to the surface of the water they are ready, it usually takes 3-4 minutes.

Drain the passatelli, place them into large bowls and cover liberally with tasty, hot meat broth. Serve them immediately.

SARDE A BECCAFICO
stuffed beccafico sardines

SERVES: 4 | PREPARATION TIME: 30 MINUTES | COOKING TIME: 20 MINUTES

This rustic sardine recipe is originally from Sicily, where you'll find many different varieties according to the area's traditions – here's my version.

FOR THE SARDINES

700g fresh sardines

12 bay leaves

1 red chilli

FOR THE STUFFING

200g homemade breadcrumbs

4 tbsp extra virgin olive oil

1 small bunch of parsley, chopped

1 lemon

2 anchovies

25g pine nuts

50g raisins, rehydrated (soaked in water)

2 tsp honey

Salt and pepper, to taste

Preheat the oven to 200°C.

Under running water, with the help of a paring knife, remove any fish scales from the skin of the sardines, and to open them up push on the belly with your thumb and gently run your finger from the belly to the tail trying to avoid breaking them. Open them out flat and clean out the guts and remove the bone. Wash delicately under cold running water and pat dry with a kitchen towel.

To prepare the stuffing fry the breadcrumbs in a large pan with a drizzle of extra virgin olive oil on low heat until golden. Add the chopped parsley, lemon zest and the anchovies. Meanwhile toast the pine nuts in a separate small pan.

Remove everything from the heat and mix well together with the chopped raisins.

Place a teaspoon of stuffing in each sardine, then roll them from head to tail.

Drizzle a bit of olive oil in a ceramic tray and place the stuffed anchovies close next to each other with a bay leaf in between each one of them.

Pour the remaining stuffing over the sardines.

Lastly, prepare a dressing with the remaining ingredients: the juice of one lemon, olive oil and the honey. Whisk well and spread it over the sardines.

Bake in the oven for 20 minutes, until the fish is cooked through and the stuffing is golden-brown. Let it rest for a few minutes and serve.

CHITARRA ALLA TERAMANA
chitarra spaghetti with tomatoes and mini meatballs

SERVES: 5 | PREPARATION TIME: 2 HOURS | COOKING TIME: 2 HOURS

This is a traditional dish from my home region of *Abruzzo*, combining fresh homemade spaghetti dressed with a rich sauce of tomatoes and lamb, veal and pork. *Chitarra* literally means guitar, because this square spaghetti was traditionally made with a machine with strings that looked exactly like a guitar. A very tasty dish for a family lunch, I strongly recommend you indulge with abundant grated *Grana Padano* cheese on top.

600g fresh pasta, (see page 214)

150g lamb shoulder, boneless

100g veal, boneless

100g pork meat, boneless

2 tbsp extra virgin olive oil

1 large onion

2 carrots

1 celery stalk

1 small bunch of thyme

1 bay leaf

1 garlic clove

½ red chilli

3 juniper berries, ground

20g butter

100ml dry white wine

1kg Imperiale d'Abruzzo tomato passata

Salt and pepper, to taste

FOR THE MEATBALLS

150g finely minced lean veal meat

1 egg

1 slice white bread, soaked in milk

Salt and pepper, to taste

4g nutmeg

Flour, to dust

Grana Padano cheese, grated, to serve

Roll out the fresh pasta with a pasta machine to 4mm thick sheets. Once the pasta starts to dry, cut the spaghetti keeping a square shape.

Season the meat with salt and pepper and roast on high heat in a large pot with a drizzle of olive oil. Once golden, add the vegetables, herbs, garlic, chilli, juniper and butter. Let it caramelise and pour the white wine in. Once the alcohol evaporates add the passata and simmer for about 1½ hours, stirring now and then.

Once the sauce is ready strain the meats and the vegetables and discard herbs, garlic and celery. Roughly chop the meats, carrots, chilli and onion and put them back in the tomato sauce.

For the mini meatballs knead together the meat with the egg and the bread well, until smooth. Season with salt, pepper and nutmeg. Make the meatballs to be between 2-4g maximum.

Dust the meatballs with flour and quickly cook them with a teaspoon of olive oil and a knob of butter. Once golden and crispy add them to the meaty tomato sauce.

Drop the chitarra in salted boiling water and cook it for about 2 minutes until al dente. Drain and toss the pasta in the meatball sauce. Stir well and serve very hot with a lot of sauce and abundant grated Grana Padano cheese.

GNOCCHI ALLA ROMANA
roman style semolina gnocchi

SERVES: 4 | PREPARATION TIME: 30 MINUTES | COOKING TIME: 30 MINUTES

An historic yet delicious classic dish from the regional cuisine of Lazio, this recipe uses semolina flour as it originates from before the 1600s, a time when potatoes weren't available in Italy. They are completely different from the traditional, more famous (and younger) potato gnocchi, in flavour, texture and looks, but they are simply delicious with their fragrant smell of roast cheese and butter.

500ml whole milk

Salt and nutmeg, to taste

35g butter

125g semolina flour

1 egg yolk

75g Grana Padano, grated

Pour the milk in a large casserole dish and bring it to simmer with a pinch of salt, very little nutmeg (be careful as it can be powerful) and a knob of butter. At this stage slowly pour in the semolina and stir well in order to avoid lumps. Cook on a low heat for about 15 minutes stirring every now and then, exactly like a polenta.

Once the gnocchi base is cooked, remove from the heat, add the egg yolk and a handful of Grana Padano and mix well until smooth.

Pour the cooked semolina in a baking tray folded with parchment and spread it evenly to a thickness of 1½cm. Allow to cool.

When the mixture is cold and firm, cut out discs with a pastry ring or a water glass about 4cm in diameter. Lift these discs out and place them in a buttered oven-safe dish or skillet, slightly overlapping them, until the dish is filled. Melt the leftover butter and pour it over the gnocchi then sprinkle them with the rest of the Grana Padano cheese.

Preheat the oven to 220°C.

Bake for 15 minutes at 180°C, until the cheese on top melts and browns. Roast the gnocchi for 5 more minutes under the grill to give them extra crunchiness, colour and a more complex flavour. Serve them while still fuming.

ORECCHIETTE CIME DI RAPA E COZZE

orecchiette with turnip tops and mussels

SERVES: 4 | PREPARATION TIME: 30 MINUTES | COOKING TIME: 25 MINUTES

Cime di rapa can be translated as turnip tops but to give you an idea it is a leafy green vegetable that looks a little like tender stem broccoli, but is much more bitter in taste. All the parts of this vegetable are edible, but the best parts are the soft buds and the little tops. This dish is traditionally made with *orecchiette*, a fun shape pasta typical in Southern Italy, especially in the *Apuglia* region. The original recipe has anchovies instead of mussels. I like to substitute salty anchovies with naturally salted mussels. The traditional recipe requires that the vegetables and pasta are to be cooked in the same water, together.

360g orecchiette pasta

300g cime di rapa (turnip tops)

200g fresh mussels

3 tbsp extra virgin olive oil

1 garlic clove, chopped

1 red chilli, chopped

100ml dry white wine

Salt and pepper, to taste

Drop the orecchiette in boiling salted water, and set the cooking time for about 12 minutes.

Trim and wash the cime di rapa (turnip tops). Remove the woody part of the stalk and keep the leaf and stem separate from each other. Once there are 8 minutes left on the timer, add the stem of the cime di rapa to the pan with the pasta. Once there are 4 minutes left, add the leaves and little tops of the cime di rapa. Keep stirring.

Rinse the mussels thoroughly, and remove any grit and beards that may be clinging to the shell. Discard any open mussels. Once the mussels are well rinsed in cold water, heat one large pan and add the extra virgin olive oil, garlic and chilli. Once it is well heated, add the mussels. Pour the white wine in, cover and let it cook for 3-4 minutes until all the mussels are open.

Once the cooking time is up, strain the pasta and vegetables. Add these to the pan with the mussels, add an extra touch of extra virgin olive oil, stir and toss well in the pan, to create a nice emulsion.

Serve hot in pasta bowls.

PASTA E FAGIOLI
pasta and beans soup

SERVES: 8 | PREPARATION TIME: 3 HOURS (PLUS OVERNIGHT TO SOAK THE BEANS) | COOKING TIME: 30 MINUTES

A very filling dish, typical of Italian countryside cuisine. From *Tuscany* to *Veneto* and Southern Italy this tasty recipe is very popular and its rustic charm has made it very successful all around the world. If you ask me the best shape of pasta for this dish it has to be the *maltagliati* which literally translates as "wrongly cut", little rough squares of pasta usually made from tagliatelle or lasagne trimmings.

We don't waste anything in our kitchen!

400g dried borlotti beans

1 pork rind (optional)

100g Grana Padano crust

1 small bunch of aromatic herbs (thyme, sage and bay laurel)

1 clove garlic, chopped

125g onion, thinly cut

125g celery, thinly cut

150g potatoes, thinly cut

200g carrot, thinly cut

100g tomato concentrate

4 tbsp extra virgin olive oil

Salt and pepper, to taste

450g fresh pasta, (see page 214)

1 small bunch of rosemary

1 red chilli, chopped

Soak the beans in cold water overnight.

Drain and cover with cold water then bring the beans to the boil slowly with the pork rind, the cheese crust, pinch of salt and pepper and a bouquet garni made of the aromatic herbs. Keep simmering for about 1½ hours. Meanwhile in a large casserole dish sweat the onion with the celery, potatoes, carrots, garlic, a drizzle of oil and a pinch of salt.

Once the beans are well cooked take out the pork rind, the bouquet garni and cheese crust.

Save some beans to use as garnish, and add the rest to the vegetables along with all of the water. Add the tomato concentrate, and let the soup simmer until the everything is soft and well cooked.

Blend well and sieve it until smooth. Add the reserved beans, season with salt and pepper to taste and keep warm and set aside.

Using a pasta maker, roll out the dough into sheets 2mm thick. Lightly flour the pasta and using a sharp knife cut the maltagliati.

Cook the pasta in salted boiling water until al dente (no more than 2 minutes) and drain straight away into the hot bean soup. If it is too thick add some cooking water.

Serve very hot with a drizzle of extra virgin olive oil, chopped rosemary and fresh chilli.

TIMBALLO DI SCRIPPELLE
timballo di scrippelle

SERVES: 4-6 | PREPARATION TIME: 2 HOURS 10 MINUTES | COOKING TIME: 1 HOUR 15 MINUTES

A great classic dish from my childhood in *Abruzzo*, similar to lasagne but instead of pasta, this recipe uses very light and thin crepes. A dish that requires time and practise, but when it is done right it will fill your heart with joy! It is ideal for a Sunday lunch or a special occasion spent with family. I deeply love this wonderfully hearty recipe, for not only is it full of flavour but also full of loving memories.

FOR THE RAGOUT

1 onion, chopped

1 tbsp extra virgin olive oil

Salt and pepper, to taste

1 carrot, chopped

1 celery stalk, chopped

1 clove garlic, chopped

Unsalted butter, for cooking

60g minced pork loin

300g minced beef

50ml dry white wine

50g tomato paste

1 small bunch of herbs (rosemary, thyme)

FOR THE CREPES

250g 00 flour

3 eggs

250ml water

250ml milk

30g unsalted butter, melted

Salt, to taste

1 tbsp extra virgin olive oil

OTHER INGREDIENTS

200g fresh large leaf spinach

1 egg

Salt and pepper, to taste

250g tomato sauce (see page 219)

300g mini meatballs (see page 80)

150g fresh peas, cleaned

250g fior di latte mozzarella, diced

200g Grana Padano, grated

40g unsalted butter

Start with the ragout. Sweat the chopped onion in a saucepan with a drizzle of extra virgin olive oil and a pinch of salt. Add the other vegetables and garlic and cook for 5 minutes. Then, add a knob of butter and the pork meat, and cook for 5 minutes. Now add the minced beef and season with salt and pepper. Cook for about 30-35 minutes until the meat has browned a bit. Pour in the white wine, and allow the alcohol to evaporate. Add a ladle full of water and the tomato paste. Then add some chopped rosemary and thyme and cook for another 15-20 minutes. Remove from the heat and set aside.

Now prepare the crepes. Combine flour with the egg, water, milk and melted butter in a blender. Blend well, add a pinch of salt and pass the mixture through a fine sieve to avoid lumps. Heat a small non–stick frying pan, with a drop of extra virgin olive oil. Use a kitchen towel to spread the oil evenly on the surface of the pan. Pour a ladle of crepe mixture into the frying pan. Allow the mixture to spread over the surface of the pan and cook 1 minute each side on medium heat. Repeat until the mixture is finished. This should make approximately 30-35 crepes. Allow the crepes to cool down on a tea towel.

Now boil the spinach and fresh peas. Cool down in iced water to retain their colour. Prepare an egg wash by beating the egg well and dressing with salt and pepper. Grease a baking tray with butter and start to lay a first layer of crepes on the bottom of the tray. Make sure the sides are also covered. Then proceed to layer with a spoon of tomato sauce, beef ragout, mini meatballs, spinach, peas, fior di latte mozzarella and a sprinkle of Grana Padano cheese. Finish with a spoon of the egg wash. Cover with a couple of crepes and repeat the operations until there are no more crepes. This will create a multi-layered lasagne-like bake. Leave a few crepes to cover the timballo. Spread a couple of knobs of butter over the top of the timballo. Bake at 150°C for 45 minutes. It will be very golden on the outside, keep an eye on the cooking after 20 minutes. If it rises too much, pierce a hole through the layers for it to reduce in size. If it is still very wobbly, allow another 10 minutes to cook and lower the temperature to 130°C.

Remove from the oven and allow to cool 10 minutes before cutting and serve.

SPAGHETTI AGLIO E OLIO CON SEDANO E PEPERONCINO

spaghetti with garlic, chilli and celery

SERVES: 4 | PREPARATION TIME: 15 MINUTES | COOKING TIME: 20 MINUTES

The extraordinary simplicity behind a plate of *spaghetti aglio e olio* actually makes it a recipe that has not been mastered by a lot of people. There is no space to hide when you've only really got three ingredients. You need to know what you're doing, and the tricks that make all the difference.

This Neapolitan recipe is a great example of Southern Italians' determination and resolution; whenever we cannot find anything more attractive than dry pasta, oil and garlic in our cupboards, we pull our resources and make a great dish out of the humble ingredients available to us.

To celebrate this great Italian classic, my version involves a personal twist. The undeniable quality of spaghetti by *Gragnano* pasta producer *Caccese*, combined with extra virgin olive oil, garlic and fresh chilli is finished off by the balance of parsley pesto and a cooling celery purée.

FOR THE PARSLEY PESTO

60g parsley leaves

10g pine nuts, roasted

40g Grana Padano cheese, grated

Salt and pepper (to taste)

80ml extra virgin olive oil

FOR THE CELERY PURÉE

50g onion, chopped

1 tbsp extra virgin olive oil

Salt and pepper, to taste

150g celery, finely chopped

FOR THE SPAGHETTI

1 slice of bread, roughly chopped

3 tbsp extra virgin olive oil

1 un-waxed lemon, zest

320g Spaghetti di Gragnano Caccese

Salt, to taste

1 clove garlic, chopped

½ chilli, chopped

Wash the parsley leaves and dry them well on a tea towel. Put them into a blender along with the pine nuts, Grana Padano, a pinch of salt and pepper and the extra virgin olive oil. Blitz quickly at the highest speed and store the pesto into a sterilised jar.

For the celery, purée sweat the onion with a drizzle of oil and a pinch of salt on low heat until it softens. Add the celery and add a ladleful of water. Cook for few minutes, blend and sieve until smooth.

Roast the bread in a saucepan with a drizzle of oil. When it's golden remove from the heat and add the lemon zest. Set aside to drain on kitchen paper.

Drop the pasta in salted boiling water, stir and cook for about 8 minutes until al dente. Meanwhile, gently heat a couple of tablespoons of olive oil in a large pan, add the garlic and chilli and cook for a couple of minutes. The garlic should be nice and golden. Drain the spaghetti and drop them in the pan with the garlic and chilli. Add 2 tablespoons of cooking water, an extra drizzle of oil and stir and toss well until creamy.

Spread the celery purée on the bottom of pasta bowls, top with a nest of spaghetti and finish with a teaspoon of parsley pesto. Sprinkle with roasted bread crumbs.

TORTELLI DI RICOTTA DOLCE POMODORO E MAGGIORANA

tortelli with sweet ricotta, tomato and marjoram

SERVES: 4 | PREPARATION TIME: 1 HOUR | COOKING TIME: 20 MINUTES

This is my personal take on a ravioli recipe from my beloved homeland, *Abruzzo*. We call it sweet ricotta because it celebrates the natural sweetness of fresh ricotta, and as a result this recipe has less salt than usual, no sugar and a touch of cinnamon. The tortelli are served with a sumptuous tomato sauce made with *passata di datterini* from *Imperiale d'Abruzzo*, grated pecorino cheese, and fresh marjoram.

250g green pasta, (see page 214)

150g tomato sauce, (see page 219)

250g fresh ricotta

Salt and black pepper, to taste

6g cinnamon powder

40g pecorino cheese, grated

2 tbsp Imperiale d'Abruzzo extra virgin olive oil

1 small bunch of fresh marjoram

Follow the recipe for the green pasta and tomato sauce on the pages listed and keep the tomato sauce warm.

Mix the fresh ricotta with a little salt, black pepper and cinnamon. Put in a piping bag.

With the help of a pasta machine, roll the pasta into thin layers. Cut some circles with a 4cm round cutter. Fill each circle with around 15g of ricotta each. Close the pasta, as ravioli or tortelli.

If the pasta is drying out while closing the ravioli, gently brush the edge of the pasta circles with water to help close the ravioli.

Cook the pasta in salted boiling water for about 1 minute and 30 seconds. Once the pasta is cooked, move onto plating. Use a pasta bowl. Spread a spoonful of hot tomato sauce on the bottom of the plate, top with ravioli, and finish with a generous amount of pecorino cheese. Drizzle with the olive oil and garnish with a few leaves of fresh marjoram.

POLIPO ALLA GRIGLIA CON ZUCCHINE ALLA SCAPECE

chargrilled octopus with courgettes alla scapece

SERVES: 4 | PREPARATION TIME: 1 HOUR (PLUS 10-12 HOURS FOR MARINATING) | COOKING TIME: 2 HOURS 15 MINUTES

Octopus is widely used across Southern Italy, and each region has its traditional method. To accompany this beautiful ingredient, I opted for a preparation called *alla scapece* with courgettes, more specifically *trombetta* courgette, which traditionally found in Naples. These courgettes are light green, longer than normal and less watery than the average courgette, so much tastier. Once thinly sliced, they are deep fried, and dressed in vinegar which was traditionally a means of keeping vegetables for longer. Nowadays, it makes for a very flavoursome recipe. It is important to remember that while cooking the octopus, the boiling should be done gently and the octopus should then be marinated in garlic, fresh herbs and chilli to bring out fuller flavours. If it is not possible to find fresh octopus, good quality frozen octopus will do just fine.

1 x 1.5kg octopus

3 tbsp extra virgin olive oil

1 sweet red chilli, chopped

½ red Tropea onion, roughly chopped

1 small bunch of fresh herbs (parsley, chives, oregano)

2 cloves garlic

4 courgettes

1 litre vegetable oil

1 small bunch of mint

50ml white wine vinegar

Salt and pepper, to taste

Fill a large saucepan with cold water.

Add the octopus. Slowly bring to a simmer for 1 hour 45 minutes. Let it cook slowly.

Check the octopus by piercing with a wooden skewer and it should be very soft. Once cooked, let it cool down in its own cooking water.

While warm, remove the octopus from the saucepan and rinse under running water. Manually remove the arms and get rid of the suckers. It is important to also clean the inside of the octopus's head.

Once clean, place in a large bowl with extra virgin olive oil, chilli, onion, fresh herbs such as parsley, chives, oregano, and a crushed garlic clove. Let it marinate in the fridge for 10-12 hours.

Now prepare the courgette. Rinse the courgettes thoroughly under running water.

With a kitchen mandoline, cut the courgette thinly.

Dress the courgette slices with salt and leave to marinate for 1 hour.

Heat the vegetable oil at 160°C in a frying pan, and proceed to fry the courgettes.

Cook until golden, then drain from the oil by placing them on a kitchen towel.

In a serving tray start to layer the courgette with leaves of mint, finely chopped garlic and drizzles of white wine vinegar. Repeat the operation until all the courgettes have all been layered.

Heat the barbecue and remove the octopus from the fridge 30 minutes prior to cooking.

When ready, roast the octopus on each side for 2-3 minutes. If a barbecue is not available, use a roasting pan.

Serve hot over the zucchini alla scapece.

BRANZINO IN CROSTA DI SALE
sea bass in salt crust

SERVES: 4 | PREPARATION TIME: 35 MINUTES | COOKING TIME: 25 MINUTES

Salt crust cooking is a very ancient method with numerous benefits. In terms of flavour, it keeps the food nice and moist, enhancing its natural flavour without adding any fat or cooking liquid. It is also a great healthy alternative to poaching or steaming.

The most common Italian salt crust recipe is with *spigola* also known as *branzino*, which you'll find in many seaside restaurants across the peninsula.

The use of whipped egg white in the crust is essential to avoid any breakages; this will help to retain all the fish's moisture.

1 small bunch of thyme	Finely chop and mix the thyme leaves, parsley and lemon zest. Scale and gut the sea bass and stuff the cavity of the fish with the herb mixture plus the smashed garlic clove.
1 small bunch of parsley	
1 lemon	
1 clove garlic	
1½ kg sea bass	Whip the egg whites and mix gently with both the rock salt and table salt until sticky. If necessary add some water.
3 egg whites	
1kg rock salt	Boil the lettuce leaves in water and pat them dry. Spread two-thirds of the mixture on the base of an oven-safe dish or skillet, brush the fish with olive oil and cover with the lettuce leaves to protect the fish. Lay the fish on the salt bed and cover it completely with the rest of the salt mixture. Press the crust firmly and make sure no spots are left without it.
1kg table salt	
1 lettuce	
2 tbsp extra virgin olive oil	

Bake at 180°C for 25 minutes.

Carefully break the salt crust, remove and place the fish meat onto a serving plate avoiding bones and fins. Season with a drizzle of extra virgin olive oil.

BACCALÀ CON BIETOLA E MAIONESE SPEZIATA

baccalà with rainbow chard and spicy mayo

SERVES 4 | PREPARATION TIME: 30 MINUTES (PLUS 12 HOURS FOR REHYDRATING) | COOKING TIME: 45 MINUTES

Baccalà translates simply as salted cod, so during cooking it is essential that you're not tempted to add any extra salt. You should also rehydrate it in running water before use.

The process used in this recipe is called confit, as the cooking will be done in immersion in extra virgin olive oil. It is really crucial to maintain the temperature at around 65°C – you don't want to fry the fish in the oil, but rather cook it gently in order to retain its moisture. Don't discard the oil used to cook the fish as it can be used to dress salads or in other fish dishes.

500g baccalà

300ml Imperiale d'Abruzzo extra virgin olive oil

1 small bunch thyme

500g rainbow chard

2 garlic cloves, chopped

2 red chillies, chopped

Sea salt flakes and black pepper, to taste

20g paprika

200g homemade mayonnaise (see page 218)

After rehydrating the baccalà fillet overnight, pat it dry with a kitchen towel and cut into 4 pieces. In a casserole dish, add the olive oil and gently place the baccalà in, making sure that the olive oil completely covers the fish, then add a bit of thyme. Cook gently for 30-35 minutes on a very low heat. With the help of a thermometer, check the temperature once in a while, making sure it does not go over 65°C.

In order to maintain the right temperature, turn the heat off every 5 minutes, then turn it on again.

While the fish is cooking, wash the rainbow chard and trim the stalk from the leaves. Do not discard the stalks. Blanch both the stalks and leaves separately in boiling salted water. Cook them separately as the stalk will take 4 minutes to cook whereas the leaves will only take 1 minute. Once they are both cooked, cool them down in iced water to retain the colour. Drain the water from the chard then in a pan fry with a tablespoon of extra virgin olive oil, a bit of garlic and a bit of chilli, then toss the rainbow chard into it. Stir fry for a couple of minutes and keep it warm.

Adjust with sea salt and black pepper to taste.

Meanwhile, to prepare the spicy mayonnaise, add a bit of chopped garlic, paprika and chilli to the homemade mayonnaise. Mix well and serve in small separate bowls for each guest. After 40-45 minutes, check the fillets by touching them gently with a finger. If the fish starts to flake apart, it means that it is very well cooked. Drain the oil from fish, remove the thyme and as mentioned before, do not discard the oil. Proceed to plating. Place the rainbow chard on the bottom of the plate and top with the baccalà. Serve the mayonnaise on the side and garnish with a little extra thyme leaves.

GELATO ALLA STRACCIATELLA
stracciatella ice cream

SERVES: 6 | PREPARATION TIME: 30 MINUTES | COOKING TIME: 10 MINUTES

Creamy *fior di latte* ice cream with flakes of crunchy chocolate. *Stracciatella* ice cream is one of the most popular and most-loved Italian ice cream flavours. I believe that this recipe is so good that you don't need anything else to accompany it!

400ml milk

150g sugar

350ml fresh cream, slightly whipped

100g chocolate (55% solid)

Bring the milk and sugar to the boil and let it cool down.

Once cold, stir in the slightly whipped cream and pour the mixture in the ice cream maker.

While the ice cream is in the machine melt the chocolate in a bain-marie and after 20 minutes, when the ice cream is almost ready, pour in the chocolate.

The cold ice cream will solidify the chocolate and the movement of the machine will shred it.

Put into the freezer to set for a couple of hours and serve as it is.

BOCCONOTTI ABRUZZESI

bocconotti abruzzesi

MAKES: 20-25 BOCCONOTTI | PREPARATION TIME: 1 HOUR 15 MINUTES | COOKING TIME: 20-25 MINUTES

This is another very traditional recipe from my region. As any ancient recipe, *bocconoti* has been adapted by different families and has spread over time to the southern part of Italy. It can now be found in many different varieties. *Bocconotto* literally means that it can be eaten in just one bite. Traditionally, the recipe is made with an olive oil shortbread pastry, filled with a *Montepulciano* grape marmalade, chopped chocolate, almonds and the cooked must of wine (*mosto cotto*). I still remember how my grandmother made these pastries; in a small aluminium mould obtained from empty olive oil tins. I love this recipe, it is a delicious treat, which is not too sweet — a perfect accompaniment for coffee.

FOR THE OLIVE OIL SHORTBREAD

250g 00 flour

1 whole egg

2 egg yolks

100g sugar

100ml Imperiale d'Abruzzo extra virgin olive oil

Sugar, to dust

Lemon, zest (optional)

FOR THE FILLING

220g red grape marmalade

100g roasted almonds

50g dark chocolate, chopped

4g powdered cinnamon

50ml Imperial d'Abruzzo mosto cotto

Start by preparing the shortbread. In a large mixing bowl, pass the flour through a fine sieve. Set aside and then beat the whole egg with the two egg yolks, then add it to the flour. Mix together then add the sugar and extra virgin olive oil. Knead all the ingredients well until it forms a smooth dough. To give the shortbread extra aroma, you can grate lemon zest inside. Wrap the dough in cling film and leave it to rest in the fridge for approximately 30 minutes.

Now, move to the filling. If red grape marmalade is not available, other jam such as blackberry or blueberry can be used as a substitute. Chop the roasted almonds and combine with the marmalade in a mixing bowl. Add the chopped chocolate, cinnamon and mosto cotto. Mix well until it makes a sticky filling.

Now, remove the dough from the cling film wrap. Cut it into slices, and roll them out into 1cm thick sheets. Cut the shortbread pastry sheets into circles with a ring, and place the circles into muffin or large cupcake moulds. The bocconotti shouldn't be larger than an espresso cup.

Add a teaspoon of filling into each circle, and proceed to cover with another circular sheet of dough of the same size. Pinch the edges to seal the dough. Repeat for each bocconotti. Let them rest for 10 minutes in the fridge.

Preheat the oven to 180°C. Remove the bocconotti from the fridge and dust them with sugar. This will result in a caramelised glaze and give the pastries an extra crunch. Bake at 170°C for about 20-25 minutes until golden. Remove from the oven and allow to cool. Serve with coffee at room temperature. The bocconotti can be stored in an air-tight container at room temperature for about 10 days.

CRUMBLE AL RABARBARO

rhubarb crumble

SERVES: 6 | PREPARATION TIME: 50 MINUTES (PLUS 3 HOURS FOR SETTING) | COOKING TIME: 30 MINUTES

I had never used rhubarb before coming to the UK but I simply love it now! Sweet and sharp, it makes the perfect match for a nutty dessert. This classic English dessert is extremely simple to make and it is for all the family to enjoy, but if you want to impress simply add some vanilla Chantilly cream and strawberry coulis and your dessert will be a huge success.

FOR THE CRUMBLE

150g butter, softened at room temperature

150g plain flour

150g sugar

150g ground almonds

FOR THE RHUBARB

500g outdoor rhubarb

100g brown sugar

100ml Moscato (sweet wine)

Icing sugar, for dusting

Preheat the oven to 160°C.

To make the crumble, soften the butter and softly rub in all the rest of the ingredients until the texture is smooth. Fold it in cling film and keep in fridge for 20 minutes to rest and firm up.

Meanwhile, wash and cut the rhubarb into short pieces (about 2cm), discard the leaves and place it on an oven tray.

Sprinkle the brown sugar on the rhubarb and pour the sweet wine in the tray.

Place in the oven for 8 minutes until the rhubarb is soft then leave to cool down.

Sprinkle the crumble on a baking tray covering every spot, put the rhubarb and its juice on top and cover unevenly with more crumble.

Turn the oven up and bake at 170°C for 15-20 minutes until golden.

Sprinkle with icing sugar and serve warm.

PIZZA DOLCE TERAMANA
pizza dolce traditional cake

SERVES: 8 | PREPARATION TIME: 1 HOUR 30 MINUTES (PLUS 3 HOURS FOR SETTING) | COOKING TIME: 45 MINUTES

This is a very traditional cake, common in the rural older parts of *Abruzzo* around the city of *Teramo*. The recipe will vary from town to town but everywhere you go in *Abruzzo,* this is the classic cake prepared for special family occasions and celebrations.

The cake is soaked in a quirky pink liquor called *Alchermes* which gives *pizza dolce* its characteristic rich sweet flavour. It is filled with vanilla custard cream and chocolate custard.

Since moving to London, there is nothing more I enjoy making (and eating) than this dish whenever I feel homesick.

FOR THE SPONGE CAKE

310g eggs

250g sugar

250g 00 flour

15g baking powder

5g salt

FOR THE ALCHERMES SYRUP

250ml water

125g sugar

½ lemon, zest

½ orange, zest

300ml Alchermes liquor

FOR THE COFFEE SYRUP

250ml water

200g sugar

250ml coffee

FOR THE CAKE

500g vanilla custard
(see bignè recipe page 136)

500g cocoa custard
(see bignè recipe page 136)

120g roasted almonds, flaked

400g whipping cream

50g icing sugar

Coffee powder, for dusting

Cocoa powder, for dusting

For the sponge cake, whip the egg yolk with the sugar in a mixing bowl until the mixture is pale and fluffy. In a different bowl, pass the flour, baking powder and salt through a fine sieve to avoid lumps. Slowly and gradually add the flour mixture to the egg yolk and sugar mixture, while continuing mixing. Whip the egg white in a separate bowl until firm, and slowly add it to the mixture. It is important to do this gently, in order to keep the sponge cake's fluffy, airy and light texture. Line a deep baking tray with baking parchment. The tray should be 3-4cm high. Pour in the sponge cake mixture. Preheat the oven to 170°C, and bake at 160°C for approximately 35-40 minutes. Make sure the door stays closed during the first 25 minutes. Once cooked, remove the golden sponge cake from oven and let it cool. Once cool, remove from the baking tray.

For the Alchermes syrup, in a saucepan combine the water with the sugar, add the lemon and orange zest. Bring to the boil. Remove from the heat, and allow to cool. Once cool, pour in the Alchermes liquor. Proceed to make the coffee syrup by combining the water, sugar and coffee. Bring to the boil. Remove from heat and allow to cool.

Cut the cake horizontally into three large slices. On the first section, brush the base with Alchermes syrup, and spread some vanilla custard over the slice. On the second section, brush the base with coffee syrup and cover the vanilla custard. Brush the top part with Alchermes syrup and spread with cocoa custard. On the bottom of the third slice of sponge brush coffee syrup and then cover the cocoa custard. Let the cake set in the fridge for approximately 2-3 hours.

Proceed to whip the cream and icing sugar until fluffy. Slice and plate the pizza dolce teramana, dust with cocoa and coffee powder, garnish with flaked roasted almonds and finish with whipped cream.

TORTA ALLA ZUCCA, MELE E CANNELLA

pumpkin and apple cake

SERVES: 10 | PREPARATION TIME: 40 MINUTES | COOKING TIME: 40 MINUTES

The use of pumpkin in desserts is becoming more and more appreciated as people begin to discover the delights of the natural sweetness of this wonderful and versatile squash. A moist and tasty cake that combines some of the most beautiful flavours that the autumn season has to offer. Don't panic if you can't get hold of a pumpkin, a butternut squash will do the job just as well. This delicious cake is perfect for a coffee break during the afternoon or even as a treat for breakfast.

1 pumpkin

3 eggs

200g brown sugar

170g 00 flour

30g strong flour

16g baking powder

100g ground almonds

150g unsalted butter, softened

4g powdered cinnamon

150g almonds, roasted and chopped

2 golden delicious apples

Start with the pumpkin purée. You'll need 300g of purée for this dish; any extra can be kept aside and used as an accompaniment for pasta, meat or fish. Remove the skin and seeds from the pumpkin and cut into rough pieces. Put the pumpkin pieces in a glass bowl and cover with cling film. Cook in the microwave for 10-12 minutes at maximum power. Once cooked, the pieces should be really soft. Put the pieces into a food processor and blend until smooth. Once ready, remove the pumpkin purée and drain over a fine sieve to remove the excess water. The purée will retain a stronger flavour by doing so.

Whisk together the eggs with the sugar for at least 5 minutes, until the mixture becomes pale and foamy. Pass the flour through a fine sieve and slowly add it to the mixture. Add baking powder and gently fold in the ground almonds. This operation must be done by hand with a pastry spatula to avoid the mixture losing air and consistency.

At this stage combine the softened butter with the pumpkin purée and the cinnamon and mix until smooth. Now gently fold the pumpkin mixture into the cake base and finally add the chopped almonds.

Line up a cake mould with backing parchment and pour in the cake mixture. Preheat the oven to 170°C. Quickly peel, trim and slice the apples to avoid them discolouring Top the cake with the sliced apples, sprinkle with some extra brown sugar and bake at 160°C for about 35 minutes. Once cooked, the cake will be golden and caramelised outside, but still moist inside. To check the cooking of the cake pierce it with a wooden skewer. If still too wet, cook for 5 more minutes.

Allow the cake to cool down and serve at room temperature. It can be stored in a cool dry place for a couple of days.

CALGIONETTI ABRUZZESI

calgionetti abruzzesi

MAKES: 50 | PREPARATION TIME: 1 HOUR 30 MINUTES | COOKING TIME: 40 MINUTES

Calgionetti Abruzzesi are sweet deep fried ravioli, made with egg-free pasta and filled with chestnuts, almonds and cocoa. Simply delicious. It is a great dairy free alternative to most pastries. These are best to be made in chestnut season, from late October until Christmas; during the festive weeks these amazing treats are always on my table.

FOR THE FILLING

500g chestnuts

20g coffee powder

50g cocoa powder

100ml sambuca liquor

½ orange, zest

½ lemon, zest

40g honey

125g roasted almonds, chopped

50g dark chocolate, chopped

FOR THE PASTA

500g 00 flour

2 tbsp extra virgin olive oil

200ml dry white wine

1 litre vegetable oil, for frying

Sugar, for dusting

Start with the filling. Roast the chestnuts in a pan on a high heat or in the oven at 220°C until they are burnt all around the skin.

Peel them and boil in water until soft.

Remove from the boiling water and mash the chestnuts while still hot.

Mash well and then combine with the coffee and cocoa powder, the Sambuca, the grated orange and lemon zest, honey, roast almonds and chocolate.

Knead well in a bowl until it creates a tough dough. If the dough is not wet enough, add a spoon of water.

Now, prepare the pasta by kneading the flour, olive oil and wine together. Make sure the dough is lump free to create a smooth and elastic pasta. If too wet, add flour.

Roll the pasta out into very thin sheets with a pasta machine.

Prepare the ravioli. Divide the filling into each raviolo, weighing approximately 15g each.

Once the ravioli are filled, cover each one with another sheet of pasta.

Heat the vegetable oil and allow it to reach 170°C.

Fry the ravioli in the oil, a couple at a time.

Turn them upside-down and as soon as they are golden all around, strain from the hot oil.

Pat dry with kitchen paper and sprinkle right away with sugar.

Serve warm or store for a couple of days and serve at room temperature.

ZABAGLIONE AL MOSCATO CON FRUTTI ROSSI

sabayon with moscato wine and mixed red berries

SERVES: 4 | PREPARATION TIME: 30 MINUTES (PLUS 2 HOURS TO LET ICE CREAM SET) | COOKING TIME: 10 MINUTES

Another old classic Italian recipe, sabayon is a mixture made with egg yolk, sugar and wine, whipped and cooked in a bain-marie, resulting in an airy, smooth and creamy custard.

Traditionally, it is served warm with biscuits; the perfect dessert for the winter season. I love to serve it with mixed berries; the mild acidity of the sweet wine combines beautifully with the sharp freshness of red berries. Add a scoop of ice cream for a real spoonful of luxury.

FOR THE VANILLA ICE CREAM

4 large egg yolks

130g sugar

350ml milk

150ml double cream

½ vanilla pod

½ lemon, zest

FOR THE BERRY SAUCE

200g mixed berries

50g sugar

FOR THE SABAYON

4 egg yolks

100g sugar

120ml Moscato wine

Start by making the ice cream. In a mixing bowl, combine the egg yolk with the sugar and whisk well until pale and foamy. Meanwhile, warm the milk and double cream in a saucepan with the vanilla pod and lemon zest. Slowly pour the warm milk on top of the egg mixture. Heat the mixture in a saucepan, and allow the temperature to reach 80°C, whilst constantly mixing.

Remove from the heat, allow it to cool and put into an ice cream maker. Once ready, after approximately 30 minutes, let it set in the freezer for a couple of hours.

Now, prepare the base for the sabayon. Wash the berries thoroughly and discard any excess leaves or stems. Put the berries in a saucepan with 50g of sugar. Put on high heat and allow to simmer for approximately 10 minutes, until the berries soften and create a thick sauce. Remove from the heat.

Aside, bring a saucepan full of water to simmer. In a large bowl, whisk the egg yolk well and slowly add the sugar, keep whisking and proceed to add the wine. Place the bowl over the saucepan full of water, and cook bain-marie. Remember, when cooking in a bain-marie method the water must never reach the boiling point as the heat would be too strong for the egg.

Whisk the sabayon thoroughly while cooking until it creates a foam-like consistency. Continue to whisk the mixture, while the egg slowly cooks in bain-marie. In a few minutes, the consistency of the sabayon will become less airy and more creamy. Remove from the heat. Put the cooked berries into small heat-proof bowls. Pour the sabayon over the berries. Place the bowls under the grill until the sabayon is golden and caramelised. Serve hot topped with a scoop of vanilla ice cream.

PIZZA DI PASQUA ABRUZZESE

pizza di pasqua abruzzese

SERVES: 8 | PREPARATION TIME: 2 HOURS (PLUS OVERNIGHT TO REST) | COOKING TIME: 50 MINUTES

The name recalls a classic flat and crispy pizza, but the appearance of this pie is quite far from it!

This particular recipe involves yeast and flour as a bread would do. It is a very ancient dessert from *Abruzzo*, a sponge-like, sweet bread which is traditional during the Easter holiday. This reminds me of past days of celebrations; it was originally a three-day recipe which has been passed along from my grandmother to myself. It can be enjoyed for breakfast, after a meal or with coffee. The secret is in the prolonged kneading of the dough, and allowing to rise properly.

Today's recipe is a faster and easier version of the traditional lengthy original.

150g dried raisins

120ml Anisetta anise liquor

200ml milk

25g fresh yeast

250g Manitoba strong flour

6 eggs

130g sugar

100g unsalted butter (softened)

250g 00 flour

1 tbsp honey

5g anise seeds

1 orange, zest

1 lemon, zest

5g powdered nutmeg

A pinch of salt

Soak the raisins into the anise liquor and leave for a couple of hours.

In a saucepan, lightly warm the milk and melt the fresh yeast inside. Pass the flour through a fine sieve to avoid lumps. In a small bowl, pour the warm milk and yeast and add 100g of the Manitoba flour. Mix it well until smooth.

Cover with a tea towel and let it rest for 45 minutes.

Aside, whisk the eggs with the sugar in a mixing bowl until pale and fluffy. Gently fold the dough into the egg mixture.

When the dough is uniform, keep kneading and add the butter, the rest of the flour, the honey, the liquor with raisins, the anise seeds, orange and lemon zest until all is fully integrated into the dough and smooth.

Let it rest overnight in a large bowl and cover with a tea towel.

The following day, grease a deep cake mould.

Before putting the dough into the mould, work the dough to remove the air inside.

Then put it into the mould and let it rest for 1 to 1½ hours in a warm room to prove.

The dough should double in size and reach the height of the cake mould.

Preheat the oven to 180°C and bake at 170°C for 45-50 minutes.

The pizza di pasqua will be very brown outside, so check the inside with a wooden skewer. If it is still too moist inside, cook for another 5-10 minutes.

It is better to lower the temperature of the oven if you are uncertain and cook the Pizza di Pasqua for longer.

Do not open the oven for the first 20-25 minutes of baking as this will interrupt the rising of the pizza and knock out all the air and fluffiness from it.

RICEVIMENTI E APERITIVI

Receptions and cocktail parties

In Italy we never drink on an empty stomach so when having a party or more formal drinks reception, we offer small bites, snacks and small dishes. It's always nicer to have freshly made food with a drink, rather than just offering nuts or crisps.

The recipes in this section are predominately smaller versions of dishes – everything is bite-sized as no cutlery is involved during events of this kind at the embassy. These can be anything from the launching of a project or initiative to a charity event, and they always offer the perfect opportunity for people to network.

Without a doubt the most popular aperitivi include the small arancini and pizzetta. They are very traditional, and loved in Italy all over.

Finally, it wouldn't be a cocktail party without a drink, so for us, prosecco is an absolute must. Salute!

BURGER DI MELANZANE
aubergine hamburger

MAKES: 12 | PREPARATION TIME: 30 MINUTES | COOKING TIME: 15 MINUTES

A lovely vegetarian alternative to the classic burger, these unusual aubergine burgers are very tasty and they make the perfect canapé choice for a summer cocktail party.

2 large aubergines

Salt and pepper, to taste

1 small bunch of thyme

3 tbsp extra virgin olive oil

170g fresh ricotta

100g Grana Padano cheese, grated

1 egg

1 tbsp homemade breadcrumbs

12 panini al latte (milk bread rolls), (see page 212)

10 cherry tomatoes

1 small bunch of basil

Preheat the oven to 180°C.

Wash and peel the aubergines, cut them into rough cubes and add salt and pepper. Roast in a frying pan with the thyme and a drizzle of extra virgin olive oil. Once cooked, remove the thyme and chop the aubergines into a paste to create a purée.

Mix the aubergine pulp with 150g ricotta, the Grana Padano and the egg.

Season to taste.

If the mixture is too soft to be worked add a spoonful of breadcrumbs.

Make the burgers no bigger than 20g and gently coat them with breadcrumbs. Roast them in oven for 8 minutes on a greaseproof tray.

Prepare each small bun, or panini al latte, with a spread of ricotta, a burger, half of cherry tomato and a basil leaf.

Roast the burgers again to give them a crunchy texture.

Serve hot with bamboo sticks.

PANE BURRO E ACCIUGHE
Bread, butter and anchovies

SERVES: 4 | PREPARATION TIME: 10 MINUTES | COOKING TIME: 4 MINUTES

The key is to use good bread for this traditional starter or canapé dish; I recommend *Pugliese* bread or a sourdough made of durum flour. The combination of roasted bread with the soft creaminess of butter and saltiness of the anchovies prepares your palate for a plentiful meal.

4 slices Pugliese bread (sourdough with durum flour)

125g unsalted butter, softened

30g anchovies

10g capers

1 tbsp extra virgin olive oil

1 orange

1 lemon

Black pepper, to taste

½ garlic clove (optional)

1 small bunch of fresh herbs

Cut the bread to the size you require and ensure the butter is at room temperature.

Drain the anchovies. Put the anchovies and capers into a food processor and mix well until almost smooth.

Add the butter, olive oil and zest of the orange and lemon into the mixture.

Whip until it becomes smooth and creamy. The butter should become white and fluffy.

Add the juice of half of the lemon.

Add pepper and garlic to taste and the fresh chopped herbs.

Put in a pastry bag.

Toast the bread at 220°C for 3-4 minutes.

Spread the anchovy butter on the warm bread.

GAMBERI ROSSI DI SICILIA CON BURRATA E PEPERONCINO
sicilian red prawn with chilli and burrata mousse

SERVES: 4 | PREPARATION TIME: 15 MINUTES | COOKING TIME: 1 MINUTE

I adore the sweetness of red prawns, especially when paired with the tanginess of chilli and the richness of *burrata* cheese. A very simple recipe, this dish relies solely on good and fresh ingredients.

FOR THE BURRATA MOUSSE

2g edible gelatine leaf

25ml double cream

125g burrata (1 burratina)

Salt and pepper, to taste

FOR THE PRAWNS

16 small Sicilian red prawns

2 tbsp extra virgin olive oil

1 tsp fresh lemon juice

1 small red chilli, chopped

1 small bunch of basil

Asparagus tops, to garnish (optional)

For the burrata mousse, soak the gelatine in cold water and gently heat the double cream. Once the cream is warm, melt the gelatine inside. Blend the cream with the burrata and season with salt and pepper to taste. Put into a pastry bag.

Clean the prawns, peel and de-vein. Prepare the dressing by mixing the extra virgin olive oil with lemon juice and chilli. Halve the prawns and dress. Season to taste.

Plate on curly spoons and top with a generous drop of burrata mousse. Garnish with fresh basil leaves or asparagus tops.

TARTAR DI MANZO
beef tartare

SERVES: 4 | PREPARATION TIME: 10 MINUTES | COOKING TIME: NONE

An extremely simple yet delicious idea for a canapé based on one of the most iconic dishes of *Piedmont's* culinary tradition. Serve it on little spoons with shaved truffle, accompanied with a bubbly glass of prosecco DOC.

200g lean cut of high quality beef, chopped (or minced)

1 large anchovy

5g capers, chopped

20g shallot, chopped

2 tbsp extra virgin olive oil

Salt and pepper, to taste

Mix all the ingredients well in a bowl and dress with oil, salt and freshly ground pepper to taste. Arrange the raw meat on curly spoons and garnish them as you like. This dish is elevated even further when paired with shaved Grana Padano cheese, fresh rocket leaves or a soft boiled quail egg with truffle.

ARANCINE POMODORO E MOZZARELLA
crispy rice balls

MAKES: 60 RICE BALLS | PREPARATION TIME: 1 HOUR 15 MINUTES | COOKING TIME: 20 MINUTES

Who doesn't love *arancine*? Crunchy and flavoursome, these stuffed rice caskets are traditionally from Southern Italy, from the wonderful region of Sicily. There are plenty of versions of arancine, which differ in stuffing and shape. My recipe is slightly different, as I have chosen to serve it as a vegetarian canapé, with tomato and mozzarella. It is the perfect canapé for a cocktail party. Save yourself some time by preparing ahead of time, as they can be stored in the freezer.

FOR THE ARANCINE BALLS

500g Riso Gallo arborio rice

20ml dry white wine

1 litre vegetable stock

250g tomato sauce (see page 219)

50g unsalted butter

60g Grana Padano, grated

2 eggs

150g fior di latte mozzarella, diced

Salt and pepper, to taste

TO PANÉ

Flour, to dust

4 eggs, for the egg wash

200g breadcrumbs

1 litre vegetable oil, for deep frying

In a large pan, start to cook the rice on a low heat, without adding oil or fat. This way, the heat reaches the core of each rice grain resulting in a more al dente texture. Keep stirring, so the grains do not catch on the bottom of the pan. When the rice is hot, pour the white wine in. Let the alcohol evaporate and add the stock a ladle at a time. Set the cooking time to 15 minutes, adding the stock little by little. Stir the rice occasionally, and keep cooking.

Halfway through cooking, add the tomato sauce to the rice. Once the time is up, taste the risotto, and remove it from the heat. Start the mantecatura as usual; add the butter, Grana Padano and eggs. Stir well to increase the creaminess of the rice. Once the rice is cooling down, add the diced fior di latte mozzarella and salt and pepper to taste. Let the risotto cool down in a large baking tray.

With the help of an ice cream scoop, start to make small balls of rice, around 30g each. Keep in the fridge for 30 minutes to allow the arancine to harden. Dust with flour and pass them through the egg wash. Roll in breadcrumbs, ensuring the whole surface is covered. For a thicker crust, repeat the process.

Deep fry in vegetable oil at 170°C, until golden. Season with a bit of extra salt, and serve hot.

BONBON CAPRINO E NOCCIOLE
goat's cheese bonbon with hazelnut

SERVES: 6 | PREPARATION TIME: 15 MINUTES | COOKING TIME: NONE

This dish is a perfect canapé for dinner parties, as a small bonbon made with soft, creamy goat's cheese covered in crunchy hazelnut with subtle sweet notes of beetroot from the powder.

200g soft goat's cheese

50g roasted hazelnut, chopped

10g beetroot powder (see page 174)

Roughly chop the goat's cheese and put into a food processor.

Once blended, it should be soft and creamy.

With your hands, create small balls, no bigger than 40g.

Coat the balls with chopped hazelnut by rolling each ball into the roasted hazelnut.

Dust the bonbons with beetroot powder, covering them all over.

Set in the fridge for 20 minutes.

Serve on bamboo sticks.

CROSTINI AI FEGATINI

chicken liver pâté crostini

SERVES: 4 | PREPARATION TIME: 30 MINUTES | COOKING TIME: 10 MINUTES

A traditional regional recipe from *Tuscany*. Tasty chicken liver pâtè crostini made with toasted *Tuscan-style* bread. A wonderful hearty dish usually served as starter but in a small version is a great canapé.

250g chicken livers

1 tbsp white wine vinegar

½ onion, chopped

1 tbsp extra virgin olive oil

Salt and pepper, to taste

40g butter

1 small bunch of fresh herbs (thyme, sage and bay leaf)

100ml Vin Santo (or sweet wine)

1 anchovy

1 tsp capers

4 slices Tuscan (or sourdough) bread

Black pepper

Chives, chopped

Carefully clean the chicken livers, then dice and soak in cold water with a splash of vinegar for 1 hour to diminish the strong flavour.

Sweat the onion in a pan with olive oil and a pinch of salt for 5 minutes. Season the livers with salt and pepper and add them in the pan. Cook the livers until pink on a high heat, for about 4 minutes, until lightly coloured. Add 20g of butter and the herbs. Pour in the wine and let the alcohol evaporate.

Remove the pan from the heat, discard the herbs and put the livers into a food processor with the cooking juice. Add the anchovy, 20g of butter and capers and blend until smooth.

Leave to set in the fridge for half an hour.

Preheat the oven to 200°C. Toast the bread in the oven for 3-4 minutes. They should be crispy and brown on the outside while soft in the middle.

With a pastry bag spread the pâté over the croutons. Sprinkle with black pepper and chopped chives. This is perfect served with caramelised shallots.

PIZZETTE
pizza bites

SERVES: 4 | PREPARATION TIME: 40 MINUTES (PLUS 2 ½ HOURS PROVING TIME) | COOKING TIME: 5 MINUTES

Who doesn't love pizza? The perfect aperitivo recipe. Small and easy to prepare, these fragrant and tasty pizzette are simply a treat you can't say no to.

8g fresh yeast

125g milk

250g flour

16g unsalted butter, softened

18ml extra virgin olive oil

10g salt

2g sugar

100g fior di latte mozzarella, diced

FOR THE TOMATO PIZZAIOLA SAUCE

200g Imperiale d'Abruzzo tomato passata

2 tbsp Imperiale d'Abruzzo extra virgin olive oil

5 basil leaves, chopped

1 tsp dry oregano

Salt and pepper, to taste

Melt the yeast in the milk then knead all the ingredients together (except for the mozzarella) until you have smooth and elastic dough. Cover the dough with a tea towel and let it prove for about 2 hours.

Meanwhile prepare the tomato sauce by simply mixing all the ingredients together and seasoning to taste. You don't need to blend your sauce but make sure everything is well mixed.

Once the dough has doubled in size the proving time is up. Roll it out with a rolling pin into a 1cm thick sheet and let it rest on the table for at least 5 minutes. During this step try not to overwork the dough as it will become too elastic. Cut with a pastry ring into discs of 3cm and place the pizzette on a baking tray with parchment. Let them rise for 30 more minutes.

Preheat the oven to 230°C.

Press the middle of the raised pizzette and add a teaspoon of pizzaiola sauce. Bake for 3 minutes at 220°C then add a few cubes of mozzarella for each pizzetta and cook for 2 more minutes until the mozzarella is well melted. Serve them hot.

BISCOTTI AL GRANA PADANO
grana padano cookies

SERVES: 4 | PREPARATION TIME: 35 MINUTES | COOKING TIME: 8-10 MINUTES

Need an idea for an aperitif at home? Here's an extremely easy option that's a great alternative to ordinary nuts and crisps. These tasty and crumbly *Grana Padano* cookies are very rich in cheese flavour, perfect as a snack for hungry dinner guests!

Make them in advance and store them for up to a week in an airtight container.

100g unsalted butter, softened

120g plain flour

120g Grana Padano cheese, grated

Knead the butter at room temperature with the flour and Grana Padano cheese until soft and smooth. Roll out the mixture over two baking sheets until 0.5cm thick. Rest in the fridge for 30 minutes.

Preheat the oven to 180°C.

With a round pasta cutter, a cookie cutter (or even a glass) cut the dough and place on a baking tray covered with baking paper.

Bake in the oven for 8 minutes until golden.

Serve at room temperature.

FRUTTA CARAMELLATA
venetian caramelised fruit

SERVES: 4 | PREPARATION TIME: 20 MINUTES | COOKING TIME: 20 MINUTES

It may sound strange but caramelising fruit is an old tradition from the region of *Veneto* and if you're lucky enough you can still find the odd peddler who sells caramelised fruit on skewers in neighbourhood fairs.

It is a simple process, but you need to be careful to get the caramel right. Humidity is caramel's enemy, so it is very important to watch the humidity level in your kitchen.

Traditionally, caramelised fruit is served as whole fruits or skewers covered in liquid caramel.

I prefer to serve them on a stick, like a lollipop, as it adds character to the fruit and is more pleasing to the eye. It is nice to have a varied selection of fruit, mixing both fresh and dried.

8 strawberries

8 white grapes

8 red grapes

8 dried apricots

16 blueberries

8 physalis

8 walnuts

FOR THE CARAMEL

150g sugar

75ml water

30g glucose syrup

Wash the fruit and allow it to dry well on a tea towel – remember water is caramel's enemy.

Start preparing the caramel. Put all ingredients into a small saucepan on a medium heat. With a kitchen thermometer, allow the temperature to reach 145°C.

Meanwhile, prepare the fruit by putting each piece on a stick.

Once the caramel is ready, remove from heat.

Dip each fruit into the hot caramel, covering the whole surface. Do this process quickly, as the caramel will become hard as soon as it cools down. In doing so, thin strings of caramel will drop off the fruit stick, this is normal.

It is helpful to have a styrofoam board or something similar to hold each stick up straight as you continue this process for all of the fruit.

Wait a few moments for the caramel to set on the fruit.

Serve within a few minutes.

BIGNÈ CARAMELLATI
caramelised choux bun

MAKES: 120 SMALL CHOUX BUNS | PREPARATION TIME: 45 MINUTES | COOKING TIME: 30 MINUTES

This is a classic; great as a petit four or served with coffee. Any filling will do beautifully; vanilla, custards, pistachio or chocolate. It is important to allow the choux pastry to rise properly, in order to fill them. I usually like to caramelise some choux buns with icing sugar and dip the others in melted chocolate. This gives them an extra crunch.

The quantity of choux buns will depend on your preferred size for each one, but don't worry, once cooked, they can be kept in the freezer. Remember, when defrosted the choux puffs need a couple of minutes in the oven to bring back their crunchiness.

FOR THE VANILLA CUSTARD

6 egg yolks

100g sugar

500ml milk

50g 00 flour

½ lemon, zest

½ orange, zest

½ vanilla pod, seeds

FOR THE COCOA CUSTARD

500ml milk

3 egg yolks

100g sugar

50g cocoa powder

50g 00 flour

60g unsalted butter

FOR THE CHOUX PASTRY

380ml water

4g salt

120g butter

25g sugar

340g 00 flour

6 eggs

Icing sugar, to dust

For the vanilla custard, whisk the egg yolks with the sugar. Meanwhile, warm the milk. Slowly add the flour through a sieve into the egg mixture and mix well. Gradually add the warm milk. Add the lemon and orange zest, followed by the seeds of the vanilla pod. Allow to simmer, and bring to the boiling point. Cook for a few minutes, stirring to avoid any lumps. Remove from the heat and put on a tray. Cover with cling film and leave to cool down.

Repeat the same process for the cocoa custard. Warm the milk and beat the egg yolks with the sugar and butter. Slowly add the flour and cocoa powder through a sieve into the egg mixture and mix well. Add the ingredients to the saucepan and bring to boiling point. Stir continuously. Remove from heat and put on a tray. Cover with cling film and leave to cool down.

For the choux puffs, combine the water with salt, butter and sugar in a casserole dish. Bring to boiling point until the butter has melted completely. Pass the flour through a fine sieve and add it gradually to the saucepan. It will form a tough dough.

Cook well for 6-8 minutes. Remove from the heat and let it cool down.

On a working surface, slowly add the eggs one at a time to the dough, kneading it well. Once the first egg has been incorporated into the dough, repeat for all the other eggs.

Preheat the oven to 200°C.

Put the pastry dough into a piping bag. Line a baking tray with parchment. Create small choux puffs. Ideally, they should be between 10-15g each.

Gently dab the top of each choux puff with a drop of water.

Bake at 180°C for 15 minutes until golden.

Remove from oven and dust with icing sugar.

Proceed to caramelise them with the grill. Keep your eye on them so they do not burn.

Let them cool down. Once cool, pierce a whole in the bottom of each choux puff and fill with the custards.

CANTUCCI ALLE MANDORLE
almond cantucci

SERVES: 12 | PREPARATION TIME: 1 HOUR | COOKING TIME: 25 MINUTES

Most people will have had *cantucci* before – they are often known as *biscotti*. These traditional *Tuscan* biscuits are usually hard and crunchy making them ideal for dipping into *Vin Santo* wine, as is ritual. However I can guarantee you that with this recipe you do not need to dip them as they are extra crumbly and good enough to be eaten at any time of the day!

Whipping the butter with sugar until really soft and creamy really helps to make cantucci more crumbly.

180g butter

350g sugar

4g salt

4g nutmeg

5g baking powder

200g eggs

500g flour

300g roasted almonds

Preheat the oven to 180°C.

Whip the butter with sugar until smooth and pale. Combine with salt, nutmeg and the baking powder. In a separate bowl, beat the eggs and add to the mixture a spoonful at a time. Fold in the flour slowly to prevent lumps, then add the almonds.

The mixture should be quite soft. With a pastry bag form into long cylinders on a baking tray covered with baking paper and bake in the oven for 20 minutes.

Remove the cantucci from the oven and, when they are cool enough to handle, slice into 1½cm rounds.

Pop the biscuits into the oven and toast them at 160°C for 5-6 minutes until golden all around and crumbly.

Once cold you can keep and store them for more than a week in an airtight container.

When we have lots of guests it is always easier to cater in buffet style. When we host a concert, exhibition or large charity event you need to plan the menu in advance very carefully as you do not know any of your guest's preferences, or if they have any dietary requirements. With such a volume of dishes, your preparation needs to be exact, and there are lots of things to take into account. For instance you have to keep in mind that most guests will be standing, so everything needs to be practical.

PRANZI A BUFFET
Buffet lunches and dinners

A couple of occasions I remember for this style of service were an important fundraising concert with Maestro Antonio Pappano and a very interesting lunch with Italian actor Toni Servillo and the whole theatrical company, when the fun upstaged the food! Guests can range from actors to designers, diplomats and athletes, so it is always a very exciting affair.

Our approach is to showcase the best of regional Italian cuisine, with a little twist and personal touch to refine the dishes. Of course there is always space for fresh bread and Italian cold cuts like culatello, as well as pasta and risotto.

For use at home, I'd recommend keeping some of these recipes in mind for when you may have visitors you don't know so well, if you're entertaining more than expected or simply if you're having a big lunch. They're great for those days when you don't want to serve and would rather everyone just help themselves!

INSALATA DI FINOCCHI ARANCE E OLIVE

fennel salad with oranges and olives

SERVES 4 | PREPARATION TIME: 15 MINUTES

This refreshing dish of Sicilian heritage made with season winter ingredients is perfect as a side salad or a starter.

The sourness of the oranges and the saltiness of the olives combined with the crispy fennel is a perfect marriage for great taste and simplicity.

4 small fennel bulbs

2 Sicilian blood oranges

10 black olives, pitted

2 tbsp Imperiale d'Abruzzo extra virgin olive oil

Salt and pepper, to taste

1 bunch of fresh herbs (basil or wild fennel)

Trim off and discard the fennel stalks. Cut the fennel in thin slices of about 2mm with the help of a mandoline slicer and leave in iced water for 10 minutes to give it a crispier texture.

In the meantime trim and slice the orange with a small paring knife and remember to save the juice to season the salad.

Drain and dry the fennel with a paper towel, then place in a bowl with the oranges and the olives. Season with drizzle of olive oil, the orange juice, salt and ground pepper to taste.

Garnish with wild fennel or fresh basil and serve in an attractive bowl.

FARINATA DI CECI
ligurian chickpea focaccia

SERVES: 4 | PREPARATION TIME: 15 MINUTES (PLUS 5 HOURS TO REST) | COOKING TIME: 30 MINUTES

This delicious and traditional recipe is from the wonderful *Liguria*. It is a sort of thin pie or flat *focaccia* made with chickpea flour, water, extra virgin olive oil and salt. You can serve it as a gluten free alternative instead of bread or simply as a tasty starter.

I advise to use a non-stick baking tray or baking parchment as you will use less oil and the *farinata* will be lighter and less greasy.

500ml water

175g chickpea flour

50ml Imperiale d'Abruzzo extra virgin olive oil

5g salt

1 small bunch of rosemary

Pepper, to taste

Put the water in a large bowl. Slowly add in the chickpea flour, mixing it with a wire whisk. Cover and leave to rest in the fridge for 5 hours. Mix now and then.

Preheat the oven to 220°C. Remove the foam from the top of the chickpea mixture. Add the oil and salt to the mixture.

Fold a large and shallow baking tray with parchment, pour in the chickpea mixture (no more than 1½cm thick) and bake in the oven at 200°C for 30 minutes, until golden and crispy on the outside. Use the grill for the last 5 minutes.

Slice it up and serve it hot, with chopped rosemary and freshly ground black pepper.

Perfect the next day if reheated.

INSALATA DI SPINACI, UOVA, PANCETTA E NOCCIOLE

baby spinach salad, with soft boiled egg, crispy pancetta and roasted hazelnut

SERVES: 4 | PREPARATION TIME: 15 MINUTES | COOKING TIME: 8 MINUTES

This is an extraordinarily simple, yet extremely tasty recipe. A versatile dish, it makes for a wonderful starter, side course or as an antipasti to share. Using the right fresh ingredients, this recipe will bring some superb flavours to life.

400g fresh baby spinach

4 eggs

8 thin slices of Italian pancetta arrotolata (rolled)

30g roasted hazelnut, roughly chopped

2 tbsp extra virgin olive oil

1 tbsp balsamic vinegar of Modena

Salt and pepper, to taste

Wash the baby spinach and let them dry on a tea towel. Cook the eggs in boiling water for 5 minutes, for the egg yolk to still be runny. Immediately put in iced water then peel carefully when cool enough to handle. Roast the pancetta slices in the oven (without fan) at 180°C for 7-8 minutes until golden and crispy. You may also use the grill if available.

To plate, in a large bowl, first place the baby spinach. Top with an egg cut in half. Cover the salad with crispy pancetta and finish with the roughly chopped roasted hazelnut. Dress with a drizzle of extra virgin olive oil, balsamic vinegar and pinch of salt and black pepper to taste.

INSALATA DI FARRO E CECI CON RICOTTA SALATA

chickpea and spelt salad, with hard ricotta cheese

SERVES: 4 | PREPARATION TIME: 40 MINUTES (PLUS OVERNIGHT FOR SOAKING CHICKPEAS) | COOKING TIME: 1 HOUR 30 MINUTES

Chickpea, spelt and ricotta are typical ingredients of central Italy's farming culture. This rustic and healthy salad is a great vegetarian alternative in a buffet-style dinner. It is also a fantastic option as a fulfilling one course meal: the spelt is a good carbohydrate, you gain all the necessary protein from the chickpeas and who doesn't love cheese with fresh tomatoes and basil? Furthermore, don't underestimate the use of fresh herbs, it adds lightness to the dish and extra layers of flavours. It really makes a difference.

I love this recipe so much that it is now a must in all buffet meals planned by me.

100g dry chickpeas	Wash the chickpeas under running water and leave to soak overnight.
Salt and pepper, to taste	To cook the chickpeas, cover them with water in a saucepan.
1 onion	Bring the chickpeas to the boil with a drizzle of extra virgin olive oil, a pinch of salt and black pepper, the onion, carrot, celery stalk, bay leaf and garlic clove.
1 large carrot	
1 celery stalk	
1 bay leaf	Adding the crust of the Grana Padano is optional at this stage.
1 clove garlic	Let it simmer for 1 hour 15 minutes until the chickpeas are well cooked. Set aside to cool down.
100g Grana Padano crust (optional)	
200g spelt	Meanwhile, rinse the spelt under running water and cook in salted boiling water for approximately 12 minutes. Cool in iced water.
200g cherry tomatoes	
3 tbsp extra virgin olive oil	Discard all vegetables and herbs from the chickpeas. Drain from its cooking water. Combine the spelt with the cooked chickpeas.
1 tbsp balsamic vinegar of Modena	
1 small bunch of basil	It is not necessary to remove the skin of the chickpeas.
150g salted hard ricotta cheese	Cut the cherry tomatoes into quarters and add to the salad. Dress with extra virgin olive oil, balsamic vinegar, a pinch of salt and pepper (to taste) and fresh basil.
1 small bunch of fresh herbs (e.g. parsley, chives, dill)	Plate in a shallow bowl. Grate the salted ricotta on top and garnish with fresh herbs.

FIORI DI ZUCCA RIPIENI
stuffed courgette flowers with mozzarella, ricotta and anchovies

SERVES: 4 | PREPARATION TIME: 15 MINUTES | COOKING TIME: 5 MINUTES

Courgette flowers are the perfect summer starter or afternoon snack. You can find similar recipes all around Southern Italy but the use of mozzarella and anchovies are most traditional around Rome area. A beautifully crunchy courgette flower, creamy cheesy filling with the intense saltiness of anchovies; what more do you want from a starter?

12 courgette flowers

250g fior di latte mozzarella

250g fresh ricotta

Salt, to taste

12 small anchovies

1 litre vegetable oil

FOR THE PASTELLA (ITALIAN BATTER)

200ml ice cold sparkling water

Salt, to taste

100g of 00 flour

1 egg white, whipped

Extra flour, for dusting

Gently trim the courgette flower from the stalk and the pistil. To rinse, prepare a bowl with cold water and gently wash the courgette flower. Pat dry gently. Prepare the filling by chopping the mozzarella. In a bowl, mix the ricotta with the mozzarella well. Add a pinch of salt to taste. Open the top of the courgette flower, without breaking them and with the help of a piping bag, fill the courgette flower with the cheese mixture until full. Add one anchovy per flower and seal the top by pinching the edges of the flowers until closed.

In a pan bring the oil to 180°C.

Prepare the pastella by mixing the iced cold sparkling water with a pinch of salt and the flour until smooth, and then gently fold in the whipped egg white. Dust the courgette flower with flour. Drop the flowers in the "pastella" and drain them gently. Drop them one at a time straight away into the hot oil. It is important that the "pastella" remain cold, to create a contrast of temperature with the heat of the oil. This will make the courgette flower extra crispy. Deep fry the flowers for around 2 minutes, with a maximum of 3 flowers at a time. Fry until golden and crispy. While frying, be gentle with the flower, to avoid the seal from opening. Drain them on a kitchen towel, to remove the excess oil. Add a pinch of salt, and serve hot.

MELANZANE A BARCHETTA
baked aubergine with tomato and basil

SERVES: 4 | PREPARATION TIME: 20 MINUTES | COOKING TIME: 20 MINUTES

Melanzane a barchetta is a very traditional recipe from *Campania*. It is a great alternative to the more classic and famous *parmigiana*, as it is dairy-free. Bursting with Italian flavours, these aubergine "boats" (that's what *barchetta* translates to) are ideal for summer meals and are perfect for family lunches or buffets.

2 large black aubergines

Salt and pepper, to taste

2 cloves garlic

1 tsp dried oregano

2 tbsp extra virgin olive oil

300g tomato sauce (see page 219)

1 small bunch of fresh basil

Cut the aubergines lengthways, without removing the top. Carve the inside of the aubergine with a knife, without piercing the skin. By doing so, you will create a grid of lines on the inside of the aubergine. Season with salt and leave for 30 minutes to allow water to leach out. Pat dry with a kitchen towel then season with black pepper. Cut the garlic cloves in half and rub over the flesh of the aubergines. Season with dry oregano and drizzle with extra virgin olive oil. Bake in the oven for 8 minutes at 160°C. Remove from the oven and spread the fresh tomato sauce evenly inside the aubergine. Ideally the tomato sauce should be thick and chunky. Bake at 180°C for another 8-10 minutes until very soft. The aubergine will soak up the beautiful flavours of the tomato sauce. Remove from oven and serve with fresh basil leaves.

Eat the aubergine pulp with a spoon and enjoy.

RISOTTO CON ASPARAGI E PROSECCO

asparagus and prosecco risotto

SERVES: 4 | PREPARATION TIME: 45 MINUTES | COOKING TIME: 30 MINUTES

A great classic creamy risotto with tangy asparagus and an extra acidity hit from prosecco DOC. Believe me, in its simplicity this recipe ticks all the boxes. A must for all lovers of Italian food.

20 large green asparagus

80g onion, finely chopped

2 tbsp extra virgin olive oil

280g Riso Gallo Carnaroli Gran Riserva rice

200ml Prosecco DOC

1 litre vegetable or chicken stock

40g grated Grana Padano

30g unsalted butter

Salt and pepper, to taste

1 small bunch pea shoots, to garnish

Trim off the bottom woody ends of the asparagus stalks. Peel with a potato peeler and boil in salted water for 1 minute. Cool them down immediately in iced water to retain the green color. Cut off the tips and set aside to use as a garnish. Chop the rest of the asparagus and keep them for the risotto. Blanch all the asparagus peelings and blend them with a glass of water. Keep this asparagus sauce to enhance the flavour of your risotto – nothing should be wasted in the kitchen!

Gently fry the chopped onion in a small casserole dish with a drizzle of extra virgin olive oil and a pinch of salt for about 10-15 minutes on low heat, until golden and caramelised. Set aside.

In a large casserole dish, start to roast the rice on low heat with a pinch of salt, without adding oil or fat. This way, the heat reaches the core of each rice grain resulting in a more uniform al dente texture. Keep stirring the rice, so it does not catch on the bottom of the pan and burn. When the rice is very hot, pour half of the prosecco DOC in. Let the alcohol evaporate, set the cooking time to 15 minutes and add the simmering stock a ladle at a time, little by little. Stir the rice occasionally, and keep cooking.

Halfway through the cooking time, add the onion to the rice and the asparagus sauce made with the trimmings.

Once the time is up, add the chopped asparagus, taste the risotto and if you're happy with the texture remove it from the heat.

This step is called mantecatura to make the risotto creamier increasing its natural ooziness with the right gesture and movements.

Add the Grana Padano and butter to the rice. Stir with energy to incorporate extra air. Add the remaining prosecco DOC and keep stirring until the risotto is nice and creamy. Season to taste.

Plate the hot risotto straight away and top with the asparagus tips and pea shoots as a garnish.

GNOCCHI DI PATATE CON VERDURE PRIMAVERILI, GRANA PADANO E TARTUFO ESTIVO

homemade potato gnocchi with spring vegetables, grana padano and summer truffle

SERVES: 4 | PREPARATION TIME: 2 HOURS | COOKING TIME: 50 MINUTES

Beautiful homemade gnocchi served in a cheese wheel; I cannot think of a more Italian presentation than this one. I usually serve this dish in a wheel of *Grana Padano* for big dinners or buffet lunches and it always impresses. When a wheel of *Grana Padano* is not available, this dish is equally wonderful served on its own. The summer truffle pairs beautifully with the cheese, as it has a very delicate taste which doesn't overpower the lovely combination of flavours from the spring vegetables.

FOR THE GNOCCHI

500g red skin boiled potatoes

200g 00 flour

2 whole eggs

150g Grana Padano cheese, grated

Salt, pepper and nutmeg, to taste

Durum flour, to dust

FOR THE VEGETABLES

4 green courgettes with their flower

1 large shallot, roughly chopped

200g green asparagus, peeled and roughly chopped

200g clean fresh peas

200g clean broad beans

2 tbsp extra virgin olive oil

20g unsalted butter

Salt and pepper, to taste

150g Grana Padano cheese, grated

1 small bunch of mixed fresh herbs, e.g. basil, dill, chives and marjoram

80g black summer truffle

Start with the gnocchi. Wash the potatoes and put in a saucepan full of water. Bring to the boil and cook through for approximately 45-50 minutes, depending on the size of the potatoes. Check by sticking a thin wooden skewer into a potato, making sure its centre is soft. Remove from the water and peel. Mash the potato and leave to cool down.

Knead the mashed potato well with the flour, eggs, Grana Padano, salt, pepper and nutmeg, to taste. Knead until the dough is smooth. Depending on the consistency, add flour.

The gnocchi dough should be moist but not wet. Cut small pieces of gnocchi dough. With the palm of your hand, roll the gnocchi out while dusting it with durum flour.

Then proceed to cut the gnocchi with a spatula. Put the gnocchi on a baking tray, dust with flour and set aside.

Now, move onto the vegetables. Wash the courgettes and flowers. Remove the pistil from the flowers and chop both roughly.

In a large saucepan, start to sweat the shallot with a drizzle of extra virgin olive oil and a pinch of salt.

After 5 minutes, add the courgette, asparagus, peas and broad beans. Cook for a couple of minutes.

Meanwhile, cook the gnocchi in boiling salted water for about 2-3 minutes until they start to rise to the surface. Strain the gnocchi and add them to the pan with the vegetables. Drizzle with extra virgin olive oil and a knob of butter. Season with salt and pepper to taste, then add the grated Grana Padano cheese. Remove from heat and mix well. Stir and toss in the pan until it creates a creamy emulsion.

Garnish with fresh herbs and finish off with generous shavings of black truffle. Serve immediately.

SARTÙ DI RISO
rice timbale

SERVES: 4 | PREPARATION TIME: 1 HOUR 30 MINUTES | COOKING TIME: 1 HOUR 15 MINUTES

This rich, fulfilling dish is surprisingly a traditional Neapolitan recipe – you would never think a maritime city as the birthplace of something so meaty! The Italian Ambassador and his family introduced me to this incredible dish; they absolutely love it. It is an extremely tasty rice pie, made with tomato risotto, mini meatballs, fresh peas, eggs and of course, mozzarella. Since being introduced to the dish, I have given it my personal touch and have loved cooking it ever since. The perfect *sartù di riso* is nice and crispy on the outside with melting mozzarella inside.

FOR THE RISOTTO

80g onions, chopped

2 tbsp extra virgin olive oil

Salt and pepper, to taste

250g Gallo arborio rice

20ml dry white wine

500ml vegetable stock

125g tomato sauce (see page 219)

20g unsalted butter

40g Grana Padano, grated

1 egg

FOR THE SARTÙ

Extra virgin olive oil, for brushing

20g breadcrumbs

4 eggs, hard boiled

300g fresh peas, boiled

250g fior di latte mozzarella, diced

200g cooked mini meatballs (see page 80)

Gently fry the chopped onions in a small casserole dish with extra virgin olive oil and a pinch of salt until golden and caramelised. Set aside.

In a large casserole dish, start to roast the rice on low heat with a pinch of salt and no fat. The heat will reach the core of each grain of rice, resulting in a more uniform and al dente texture. Keep stirring to prevent it from sticking the bottom of the pan. When the rice is hot, add the white wine. Set a cooking timer to 15 minutes. Add the vegetable stock little by little. Stir the rice occasionally. Halfway through the cooking time, add the cooked onions and tomato sauce. Once the time is up, taste the risotto for texture. Remove from the heat and start the mantecatura, which is the process of making the risotto creamier by increasing its natural ooziness with the gestures and movements. Add the butter, the Grana Padano and the egg. Stir well to increase creaminess. Season to taste. Let the rice settle.

Line a cake tin with baking parchment.

Brush with extra virgin olive oil and sprinkle with breadcrumbs. Fill the tin with a couple of spoonfuls of the warm risotto. Create layers of sliced eggs, peas, mozzarella and meatballs and cover with rice. Press well until it is evenly packed. Sprinkle with breadcrumbs.

Bake the sartù at 160°C for about 40 minutes until it is nicely golden and crispy. It should create a solid crust. Remove from the oven. Let it cool down for 10 minutes. Remove from the cake tray, slice and serve hot.

FRITTO MISTO ALL'ASCOLANA
fritto misto ascolana-style

MAKES: 50 OLIVES, 50 CREMA FRITTA (CREMINI) | PREPARATION TIME: 2 HOURS | COOKING TIME: 45 MINUTES

Ascoli is a wonderful ancient city close to the border between *Marche* and *Abruzzo*. Taking elements from both regions, this dish is a fried heaven of lamb, battered vegetables, sweet custard fritters and *olive all'Ascolana;* these amazing olives are stuffed with meat, breaded and deep fried to crispy perfection!

Tradition calls for this recipe to use a quality of olives called tenera ascolana, which are meaty elongated olives infused in brine with fennel and pitted by hand. The *crema fritta*, a sweet custard used in this recipe, is also breaded and fried. This is a rich course, ideal as a main. It can also be found in street food festivals, as small bites to share like my version. The recipe requires quite a long preparation time, but once the crema fritta and olives are ready, they can be stored in the freezer and kept for later use.

Let me share a secret, to this day, my mother's *olive all'Ascolana* are still unbeaten, which is hard to admit even by me!

FOR THE CREMINI

4 egg yolks
50g sugar
500ml milk
1 lemon, zest
100g 00 flour
Flour, to coat
1 egg, for the egg wash
Breadcrumbs, to coat

FOR THE OLIVE ALL'ASCOLANA

50g pork loin meat
50g lean beef meat
50g chicken meat
1 onion, chopped
1 carrot, chopped
1 celery, chopped
3 tbsp extra virgin olive oil
1 small bunch of sage
150ml dry white wine
30g mortadella di Bologna
3 eggs
Salt, pepper and nutmeg, to taste
40g Grana Padano cheese, grated
500g olive tenere ascolane
Flour, to coat
Breadcrumbs, to coat
1 litre vegetable oil

Start with the cremini. Beat the egg yolks with the sugar in a mixing bowl until pale. In a saucepan, warm the milk with the lemon zest. Pass the flour through a fine sieve to avoid lumps and add it to the egg yolk and sugar mixture. Pour the warm milk onto the mixture. Transfer the milk, sugar, egg yolk and flour mixture back to the saucepan and bring it back to the boil for about 2-3 minutes. Stir while cooking, and whisk well to avoid lumps. Once ready, remove the lemon zest and pour the hot custard onto a baking tray of 2cm deep.

Cover with cling film and let it set in the fridge for 2 hours. Once the custard is cold, cut into 3cm cubes. Dust the cubes with flour. Gently dip each cube in the egg wash, and coat with breadcrumbs. Repeat for each cube and set aside.

Now proceed to prepare the olive all'Ascolana. Start with the filling. Cut each meat into cubes and set aside. In a large saucepan, add a couple of spoons of extra virgin olive oil and start to sweat the chopped vegetables with the sage and a pinch of salt. Once the vegetables are golden, add the meat cubes and roast well. Once golden, pour the dry white wine into the saucepan.

Allow the alcohol to evaporate and keep cooking with the lid on for a few minutes. Once cooked, remove from the heat and allow to cool down. Remove the sage. When cold, mince all the ingredients into a meat mincer with my personal addition of mortadella. Place the mixture into a large bowl, add 1 egg and mix well until it creates a paste. Season with salt, pepper, Grana Padano and a touch of nutmeg. Allow to rest for 30 minutes in the fridge.

Meanwhile, remove the pit from the olives, using a small paring knife. Stuff each olive with the meat filling. Repeat for each olive. Let them rest in the fridge for 30 minutes. Dust with flour, dip into the egg wash from the remaining two eggs and coat them in the breadcrumbs.

Once finished, let them rest in the fridge for a few minutes. In a frying pan, heat the vegetable oil at 180°C and deep fry the stuffed olive and cremini.

Once golden all over, drain on kitchen paper. Season the crema fritta with sea salt and serve hot.

VITELLO TONNATO
veal with tuna sauce

SERVES: 6 | PREPARATION TIME: 1 HOUR (PLUS 12 HOURS FOR MARINATING) | COOKING TIME: 1 HOUR 30 MINUTES (PLUS 2 HOURS FOR RESTING)

This recipe is a classic from the *Piedmont* which has, quite rightly, spread throughout the rest of the country and beyond. Roast veal served pink and cold, with a sauce made of tuna, capers, anchovies and homemade mayonnaise; it makes a wonderful main course, but for me it is best served amongst a selection of antipasti to share, with lovely homemade *giardiniera* (pickled vegetables). I prefer the veal *girello* cut of meat, and I usually opt for a canned tuna in extra virgin olive oil. My take on the classic *vitello tonnato* is slightly unconventional, as I soak the veal overnight in brine and steam it. This results in a consistent veal texture which will be perfectly pink and won't lose blood when cut. It does not need to be dressed with salt and pepper.

1 X 1kg veal girello

FOR THE PICKLING LIQUID

2 litres water

150g salt

1 bay leaf

5 peppercorns

FOR THE SAUCE

250g canned tuna in extra virgin olive oil

20g capers

150g homemade mayonnaise (see page 218)

6 anchovy fillets

150g homemade giardiniera (see page 70)

1 bunch of fresh herbs (e.g. parsley, basil, chives and dill)

20g roasted hazelnuts

Start by preparing the pickling liquid. Combine all the ingredients and bring to boiling point. Then let it cool down.

Trim the veal, discarding the tough outside tissue and poach it in the pickling liquid. Make sure the veal is covered by the liquid. Allow it to marinate in the liquid for about 12 hours. Remove the veal from the liquid, pat dry with a kitchen towel and wrap in cling film. Make sure it is wrapped tightly. Set the oven to steam mode at 56°C. Put the veal wrapped in cling film into the oven and cook for 1 hour 30 minutes. If a steam oven is not available, pan-sear the veal and put it in the oven at 180°C for 15-20 minutes. Once cooked, remove from the oven and allow to cool. Let it rest in the fridge for a couple of hours.

Remove the veal from the fridge, and remove the cling film wrap. Heat a non-stick frying pan. Drizzle with some extra virgin olive oil and pan-sear the outside of the veal very quickly. This step should take only a couple of minutes; the heat must not reach the core of the meat. This step does not have to be done if you are not using a steam oven.

Optional: Add chopped onions, carrots, celery, rosemary and a knob of butter. This will give the veal an extra roasted aroma. Allow the veal to rest 5 more minutes.

Proceed to preparing the sauce. Drain the olive oil from the tuna. In a food processor, put the tuna, capers and two fillets of anchovy. Blend well until creamy and add the mayonnaise. Now slice the veal very thinly and start to plate. Dress the sliced veal with the tuna sauce. Garnish with homemade giardiniera, fresh herbs, the remaining anchovy fillets and a few roasted hazelnuts.

TORTA DI FARINA DI POLENTA E NOCCIOLE

polenta and hazelnut cake

SERVES: 6 | PREPARATION TIME: 30 MINUTES | COOKING TIME: 40 MINUTES

This is a very tasty cake, rich in nutty flavour. Made with polenta flour, it has a very low gluten level, giving it a crumbly texture. It is ideal for breakfast or afternoon tea. It would also make the perfect dessert for a dinner party if served with chocolate ganache and salted caramel.

100g softened butter

120g sugar

2 eggs

8g baking powder

50g 00 flour

100g mais corvino flour (polenta)

100g ground almonds

20g hazelnut paste

Preheat the oven to 180°C.

Whip the butter with sugar until it forms an airy white mixture.

In a separate bowl, beat the eggs. Add the eggs to the butter and sugar. Keep mixing until smooth.

Add the rest of the ingredients, one at a time, saving the hazelnut paste until last.

Avoid lumps by stirring thoroughly and adding the ingredients gradually.

Once the mixture is smooth, add the hazelnut paste.

Line a round cake mould with baking parchment. Pour in the mixture and allow for it to reach 3-4cm height.

Bake at 160°C for about 40 minutes.

Check the cake with a toothpick, if the toothpick comes out clean it is cooked. Let it cool.

Serve as it is or dust with cocoa powder.

BABÀ NAPOLETANO
neapolitan babà

SERVES: 10 MINI BABÀ | PREPARATION TIME: 45 MINUTES | COOKING TIME: 20 MINUTES

Some say the birthright of this amazing dessert belongs to a Polish king, but we all owe it to the talents of Neapolitan pastry chefs for making it famous worldwide.

I didn't always enjoy *babà* for the too strong alcohol taste until I learnt how to do my own version of it.

When I came across this recipe I was amused by how simple the method can be; I had only known very time-consuming complicated ones.

As with every bread recipe, remember to use strong flour and fresh yeast.

80g Manitoba strong flour

60g 00 flour

20g fresh yeast

140g egg yolk

40g unsalted butter, softened

3g salt

15g sugar

FOR THE SYRUP

1 litre water

500g sugar

1 unwaxed lemon, zest

½ vanilla pod

200ml Nocino liquor
(walnut flavoured liquor)

Pass the flours through a fine sieve to avoid lumps, then knead very well with the yeast, the egg yolk and the butter until you have a very smooth dough.

Make sure the yeast is well melted and only at this stage add the salt and sugar.

Grease the high moulds for babà with abundant butter (a soufflé mould will work just as well) and place 30g of the dough into each one of them. Let them rise for about 1 hour at room temperature until they have reached the edge of the moulds. Preheat the oven at 170°C and bake at 160°C for 15 minutes until golden, almost browned.

The cooking and proving time can vary by the size of your babà.

Allow them to cool and remove from the moulds.

Once you're ready to serve the babà, prepare the syrup. In a casserole dish bring the water to boil with the sugar, lemon zest and vanilla pod with the seeds scraped out.

Once the sugar has dissolved take it off the heat and add the liquor for extra flavour.

While the syrup is still warm soak the babà in it for a few seconds until soft and spongy.

Repeat if needed and let the babà drain on a rack.

This dish is great if served warm on their own, but are also amazing with whipped cream and fresh berries.

TORTA CAPRESE
chocolate and almond caprese cake

SERVES: 10 | PREPARATION TIME: 30 MINUTES | COOKING TIME: 40 MINUTES

The *torta caprese* is a traditional cake from *Campania*, and more precisely from the isle of *Capri*. As legend has it, this cake was being created by mistake, after accidentally being made without flour. What a lucky mistake – it is delicious!

Nowadays, this cake is an excellent gluten free alternative, as it uses ground almonds instead of flour. It is a very dense, with strong notes of chocolate. It has a crunchy outside shell, and a very moist inside, similar to the texture of a brownie. It can be served as it is with a dusting of icing sugar, or alternatively, with fresh strawberries and vanilla Chantilly cream.

5 eggs

200g granulated sugar

250g dark chocolate (55%)

250g unsalted butter

300g ground almonds

Whisk the eggs with the sugar for at least 5 minutes, until the mixture becomes foamy.

Meanwhile, start to chop the chocolate into small pieces with the help of a food processor.

Melt the chocolate in a bowl, over hot water. Once the chocolate has melted, remove from the heat and add the butter.

Stir until it has melted and is smooth. Once the egg mixture is well whipped, carefully add the ground almonds, avoiding creating lumps, and losing the foamy consistency.

Once the eggs and almonds mixture is smooth, slowly add the melted chocolate and butter. Mix until creamy.

Take a cake tray or a round mould and line the tray with baking parchment, then slowly pour the mixture in.

Spread it evenly.

Preheat the oven to 170°C then bake the cake at 160°C for at least 40 minutes.

To check the cake, a crust should appear on its surface, then with the help of a toothpick, check the inside, it shouldn't be runny at all, only very moist.

Once the cooking time is up, remove from the oven, and let it cool.

Unmould the cake, and put on a serving tray.

Dust with icing sugar and serve.

Here we arrive at the main event. These important dinners are always black tie and the formalities extend to the dishes we serve too. I always strive to offer a certain 'wow factor' on these occasions. The menu is meticulously planned along with wine pairing for each dish, as it needs to reflect the calibre of the event. It's a much more glamorous occasion and one where I'm able to show off a bit.

The dishes in this chapter are a bit more sophisticated and refined, involving slightly more skill. I can force my hand and be a bit more creative, as I know this will be appreciated by the guests, who more often than not will be used to a certain level of fine dining. Everyone from the likes of Valentino, Stanley Tucci, Boris Becker and even Victoria Beckham has attended a gala dinner at the Italian Embassy at some point.

PRANZI DI GALA
Gala dinners

As with all of my recipes, though they may look different they are usually a twist on something traditional; evoking a memory or element that I really like. Like a lot of Italian recipes, they may be derived from cucina povera Italiana (the cooking of the poor) and have been embellished since. The same ideas apply, but more luxurious ingredients or extra elements may also be used.

These dishes are perfect for when you want to impress guests or even just to treat yourself; everybody deserves that once in a while.

TORTELLINI DI BURRATA CON GAMBERI ROSSI DI SICILIA E BRODO DI CARCIOFI AFFUMICATO

burrata tortellini with Sicilian red prawns and smoked artichoke broth

SERVES 4 | PREPARATION TIME: 3 HOURS | COOKING TIME: 50 MINUTES

This is one of my oldest signature dishes, and one of my all-time favourites… I absolutely love Sicilian red prawns; they are incredibly sweet and they have an amazing smell. They're pretty much different from any other prawns you can find around as they are smaller in size and offer a really delicate flavour. This why I love to serve them raw.

The creamy *burrata* cheese offers a hint of acidity and the bitterness of the artichokes complements the prawns perfectly. Don't worry too much about the trick of the multicolour pasta, it is easy to get the hang of after you make a couple. The pasta recipes are on page 214.

FOR THE MULTICOLOUR PASTA

150g egg pasta

150g parsley pasta

150g squid ink pasta

150g egg white pasta

150g cocoa pasta

150g beetroot pasta

FOR THE FILLING

250g fresh burrata cheese

4g edible gelatine leaf

50g double cream

Salt and black pepper, to taste

FOR THE GARNISH

12 small fresh Sicilian red prawns

Flaked sea salt

3 tbsp extra virgin olive oil

8 medium artichokes

1 lemon, juice

200ml vinegar

1 celery stalk

1 shallot

1 clove garlic

1 lemongrass stalk

Fresh herbs

10g smoked Earl Grey tea

Basil cress to garnish

Salt and pepper, to taste

Get started with the striped pasta. Knead each kind of pasta until it is smooth and elastic and roll out with the pasta machine. Then pile up every layer of coloured pasta on top of each other as you prefer. Halve the block of pasta that you have created. Combine the first half on top of the second one until you get block of multicolour pasta ready to use. Put it in a sous-vide bag or wrap it in cling film and leave to rest for 1 hour in the fridge.

For the filling, drain the burrata from its water and put it in a food processor. Soak the gelatine in cold water and in the meantime heat the double cream. Do not bring it to the boiling. Remove the cream from the heat and add the drained gelatine leaves.

Add the mixture to the burrata and season with a pinch of salt and black pepper. Blend everything together for 1 minute. Now put the filling in a pastry bag and let it rest for about 30 minutes in the fridge.

Peel the prawns and discard the gut. Gently season them with sea salt flakes ground black pepper and a drizzle of olive oil, then leave them to marinate in the fridge.

Clean the artichokes and pull off the external hard leaves. Discard the woody part and peel the stem left with a peeler. Then trim the top if it is too hard and cut the heart in a half. Remove the "fuzzy" choke with a small paring knife.

Immediately drop the cut artichokes in cold water with lemon juice to prevent them discolouring.

In a large pot bring 2 litres of water to the boil with vinegar and a pinch of salt. Cook the artichokes in boiling water for 5 minutes. Drain and cool down.

Use all the artichoke trimmings for the smoked broth. Put them in a large pan with all the vegetables, the lemongrass and a few fresh herbs, cover with cold water add pinch of salt and bring it to the boiling. Add a couple of prawn heads and cook it for 5 minutes. Put the smoked tea in and leave it for 2 minutes. Pass it through a sieve, season to taste and keep it simmering.

Making tortellini is easier than it looks. With a pasta machine roll out the multicolour pasta so it is extremely thin. Slice the block of coloured pasta vertically to keep the striped pattern. Use a pastry cutter to stamp out small discs. Pipe a nice amount of burrata mousse in the middle of each ring.

Brush the edges around the filling with a little water, then fold the dough in half over the filling, making a half-moon shape. Be sure all the filling stays inside. Squeeze out any air, press down to seal the edges and fold them around your little finger. You may need some attempts before getting it right!

In a pot with salted and boiling water cook the tortellini for about 1 minute or until they float to the top of the pan. Meanwhile in a non-stick pan quickly roast the artichokes. To serve, in each plate arrange 3 prawns with a few pieces of artichoke and at least 8 tortellini. Garnish with fresh basil cress and drizzle over a bit of olive oil. Pour the hot smoked artichoke broth over the dish in front of your guests at the table.

PINK RISOTTO CON BARBABIETOLA, FORMAGGIO DI CAPRA E RADICCHIO TARDIVO DI TREVISO

pink risotto with goat's cheese, beetroot powder and radicchio tardivo

SERVES 4 | PREPARATION TIME: 45 MINUTES | COOKING TIME: 30 MINUTES (PLUS 6 HOURS FOR THE BEETROOT POWDER)

I love risotto and this is a successful signature dish of mine. It is perfect for an elegant dinner, as the pink colour makes it very appealing. The soft goat's cheese complements the sweetness of the beetroot and the mild bitterness of the *radicchio tardivo*, which is very different to any other kind of radicchio. You should definitely try it!

1 radicchio tardivo

10ml mosto cotto (sweet cooked grape must)

80g onion, finely chopped

25g unsalted butter

18g soft goat's cheese

280g Riso Gallo Carnaroli Gran Riserva rice

150ml prosecco DOC

1 litre vegetable or chicken stock

40g Grana Padano, grated

1 tbsp extra virgin olive oil

Salt and pepper, to taste

FOR THE BEETROOT POWDER

3 boiled whole beetroots

2 tsp icing sugar

For the beetroot powder, cut the cooked beetroot into thin slices with a kitchen mandoline or slicer. Place the slices on a baking tray, lined with baking paper. Sprinkle the slices with icing sugar. Bake for 5-6 hours at 75°C to dry the beetroot out. Once they have been dehydrated, blend and pass them through a fine sieve, to obtain a very fine powder.

Wash the radicchio and let it drain with its head upside down, removing any remaining water. Cut the leaves individually, and brush with mosto cotto. Bake the leaves at 180°C for 30 seconds only.

Gently fry the chopped onion in a small casserole dish with a drizzle of extra virgin olive oil and a pinch of salt for about 10-15 minutes on a low heat, until nice and golden. Set aside. Cut the butter into cubes, and roughly chop the goat's cheese.

In a large pan, start to roast the rice on low heat, without adding oil or fat. In this way, the heat reaches the core of each rice grain resulting in a more al dente texture. Keep stirring the rice, so the grains do not catch on the bottom of the pan. When the rice is hot, pour the prosecco in. Let the alcohol evaporate and add the stock a ladle at a time, keeping it simmering. Set the cooking time to 15 minutes adding the stock little by little. Stir the rice occasionally, and keep cooking.

Halfway through the cooking, add the onion to the rice.

Once the time is up, taste the risotto and if you're happy with the texture remove it from the heat.

This step is called mantecatura to make the risotto creamier increasing its natural ooziness with the right gestures and movements.

Add the soft goat's cheese, the Grana Padano and butter to the rice. Stir with energy to incorporate extra air. Serve the rice in large plates. Top with the mosto cotto brushed radicchio leaves and sprinkle with beetroot powder.

Serve immediately.

UOVO IN RAVIOLO SAN DOMENICO

uovo in raviolo from san domenico restaurant in Imola

SERVES: 4 | PREPARATION TIME: 45 MINUTES | COOKING TIME: 8 MINUTES

For those who aren't familiar with San Domenico in Imola, near Bologna, it is a two Michelin-starred restaurant that opened in 1970 by *Gianluigi Morini*. This establishment has made history as part of Italy's gastronomic rise, and I would go as far as saying that this restaurant is a landmark. Over the years, so many chefs have worked and trained there, and I am one of those. I have to admit, I left a piece of my heart in that kitchen. To this day, the restaurant's tradition has been kept within the same family. The renowned chef *Valentino Marcattilii* continues to work at the San Domenico with brother *Natale Marcattilii* holding reins in the dining rooms, along with the support of his nephew, the talented chef *Massimiliano Mascia*. They continue to strive for perfection every day.

On both a professional and personal level, I feel very close to this recipe, as it is an incredible dish, in all its simplicity. The dish was created in the early 1970s by an iconic chef of the time called *Nino Bergese*, former chef of Italian royalty and aristocracy. Until this day, the recipe remains unchanged; a fresh *raviolo* filled with ricotta and spinach and a whole egg yolk. The pasta is served with noisette butter, *Grana Padano* and fresh truffle. Use the truffle according to season, either winter or summer truffle to complement the dish. It is a sumptuous dish, and at the embassy we often serve as part of a gala dinner.

FOR THE FRESH PASTA

200g 00 flour

2 eggs

Pinch of salt

FOR THE FILLING

40g fresh spinach

1 tbsp extra virgin olive oil

200g fresh sheep ricotta, chopped

200g 24 months Riserva Grana Padano, grated

Salt, pepper and nutmeg, to taste

4 Italian eggs

200g unsalted butter

50g fresh truffle (according to season)

Knead the flour and eggs with a pinch of salt, until you have a smooth and elastic pasta dough. Cover with a tea towel and leave to rest for about 30 minutes. Start to prepare the filling. Wash the spinach and trim from the stalk. Cook in a pan for about 1 minute, with a drizzle of extra virgin olive oil and a pinch of salt. Remove from the heat and allow to cool down. Chop roughly and mix well with the ricotta. Add two handfuls of Grana Padano cheese, a pinch of salt, black pepper and a little grated nutmeg.

Put the filling into a piping bag. With the help of a pasta machine, roll the pasta out. Pass the dough through the narrower setting to make very thin pasta sheets. Cut the pasta in 12cm discs. Create a circle of filling in each pasta disc large enough to hold an egg yolk in the middle. Gently place an egg yolk on each disc, and sprinkle with a pinch of salt. Brush the edge of the pasta disc with water. Cover with another disc and seal the edges.

Trim the edges of the raviolo with a pastry wheel. Bring a pot of water to boil. Before lowering the raviolo into the boiling water, melt the butter on high heat in a separate casserole dish until brown. Drop the raviolo into salted boiling water. Cook for approximately 2 minutes, depending on the thickness of the ravioli. Do not cook for more than 3 minutes.

Drain after and place gently into a deep plate. Sprinkle with abundant Grana Padano, shaved truffle and finish with a nice spoonful of brown butter.

The egg yolk should be runny, giving a beautiful flavour and texture to the dish.

RISOTTO ALLE MELANZANE CON SGOMBRO MARINATO E BURRATA

aubergine risotto with mackerel and burrata cheese

SERVES: 4 PEOPLE | PREPARATION TIME: 1 HOUR 45 MINUTES | COOKING TIME: 45 MINUTES

This is an unusual creation of mine that works surprisingly well, evoking elegant and extremely tasty flavours. The smokiness of the aubergine is complemented by the tangy marinated mackerel, which is enhanced further by the flavours of the lovely *burrata* cheese, roasted tomatoes and basil.

As in every great risotto, the use of *Carnaroli* rice is recommended for the dish to be its best. This is definitely a distinctive recipe to try if you have important guests to impress; the surprising Italian flavour combinations are sure to delight!

2 large black aubergines

Salt and pepper, to taste

4 tbsp extra virgin olive oil

1 small bunch of thyme

1 clove garlic, smashed

2 ripe plum tomatoes

40g onion, chopped

280g Riso Gallo Carnaroli rice

120ml prosecco DOC

1 litre vegetable or chicken stock

40g Grana Padano, grated

20g unsalted butter

50ml white wine vinegar

150g burrata cheese

1 small bunch of basil

2 fillets marinated mackerel (see page 34)

Peel the aubergines and cut them into 3cm thick slices. Dress them with salt and set aside for a couple of hours to get rid of the bitter vegetable water. Pat the aubergine slices dry with kitchen paper. Cut a few cubes from two slices and roast in a small pan with a drizzle of extra virgin olive oil. Dress the slices left with olive oil, thyme leaves, and rub with the smashed garlic clove. Let them marinate for 1 hour. Cook the aubergines over the barbecue on low heat for about 20 minutes. During the cooking time, put a handful of wood chips into the barbecue and cover all to intensify the smokiness of aubergines. Let them cool and blend them in a food processor until smooth.

Blanch the tomatoes in boiling water, quickly cool down in iced water, peel them and cut into 4 wedges, getting rid of the seeds and watery insides. Dress the tomatoes with a drizzle of oil, salt and pepper and roast at 180°C for about 5 minutes.

Gently fry the chopped onion in a small casserole dish with a drizzle of extra virgin olive oil and a pinch of salt for about 10-15 minutes on low heat, until golden and caramelised. Set aside.

In a large casserole dish, start to roast the rice on low heat with a pinch of salt, without adding oil or fat. This way, the heat reaches the core of each rice grain resulting in a more uniform al dente texture. Keep stirring the rice, so it won't stick on to the bottom of the pan and burn. When the rice is very hot, pour the prosecco DOC in. Let the alcohol evaporate, set the cooking timer to 15 minutes and add the stock a ladle at a time, keeping it simmering. Stir the rice occasionally, and keep cooking.

Halfway through the cooking time, add the onion and the aubergine purée to the rice.

Once the time is up, taste the risotto and if you're happy with the texture remove it from the heat.

This step is called mantecatura; making the risotto creamier by increasing its natural ooziness with the right gestures and movements.

Add the Grana Padano and butter to the rice. Stir with energy to incorporate extra air. Add the white wine vinegar and keep stirring until the risotto is nice and creamy. Season to taste.

In a separate bowl break the burrata cheese by hand in rough pieces, dress it with salt and pepper to taste and add drizzle of extra virgin olive oil.

Serve the hot, creamy risotto in a large plates, top with 1 fillet of marinated mackerel divided in 4 pieces for each dish, add the warm roasted tomatoes, aubergines and the burrata cheese.

Drizzle with extra virgin olive oil and garnish with leaves of fresh basil.

ROMBO CON VARIAZIONI DI CARCIOFI
turbot with artichoke

SERVES 4 | PREPARATION TIME: 1 HOUR 15 MINUTES | COOKING TIME: 40 MINUTES

Turbot is a fantastic meaty white fish, often referred to as the "king of the sea", so it stands up very well with the bitterness of the artichokes. I strongly suggest that you ask your fishmonger to fillet the turbot beforehand for you because they are usually very large, and you will not need the whole fish. That said, the bigger the fish, the better it is! A signature dish of mine, I often use it for important gala dinners, and it has never disappointed me. The varying textures of the artichokes cooked in three different ways are what really bring this dish alive.

1 X 600g large turbot fillet

Flour, for sprinkling

9 artichokes

1 litre vegetable oil, for frying

10 parsley leaves

1 lemon, squeezed

Salt and black pepper, to taste

400ml white wine vinegar

3 tbsp extra virgin olive oil

4 spring onions

1 small bunch of thyme

1 orange

Clean the fish (and fillet it if you haven't already had it done for you). As you clean it, make sure that the fish has been boned properly.

Take one raw artichoke and cut it thinly lengthways with a kitchen mandoline or slicer if you have one. Quickly sprinkle some flour over the sliced artichoke and fry it in vegetable oil at 140°C for 4 minutes, until it is golden. Once you have deep-fried the artichokes, you can use the same oil to deep-fry the parsley leaves, at the same temperature, for about 30 seconds, until they become very crispy.

To clean the artichokes, pull the external hard leaves off and discard any woody part of the stalk. With a potato peeler peel the remaining stem. Trim the top of the artichoke, (as it is usually too hard) cut the artichoke in half, and remove the hairy choke at the centre with a small knife. As soon as you have cleaned the artichokes, drop them in cold water with the lemon juice to prevent the discolouring of the artichoke. Bring 2 litres of water to the boil, with a pinch of salt and the white wine vinegar. Cook the artichokes in the boiling water for around 4-5 minutes. Drain them and season with a drizzle of olive oil.

For the artichoke purée, you'll need to use half of the artichokes to make the purée. Thinly cut the spring onions and stew them over a medium heat with a drizzle of extra virgin olive oil, a pinch of salt, a few leaves of thyme and the orange zest (save some of this for the garnish). Once the spring onion is well cooked, add the artichokes. Add a ladle full of water and cook for about 5 minutes. When everything is well cooked, blend it and sieve it until its consistency is smooth and creamy. Season with salt and pepper to taste.

Then, with the leftover artichokes, roast them with a bit of extra virgin olive oil in a non-stick pan. Stir-fry them very quickly with a touch of salt and pepper until they are golden.

Now it's time to roast the turbot, as everything else is ready. Season the fish with salt and pepper. Heat a non-stick pan. Once the pan is very hot, start to cook the fish with a drizzle of olive oil. Allow 2 minutes per side in the pan until it is nice and golden. The fish should become a little bit crispy on the outside. It is up to you whether you like your fish with the skin on or off, I usually remove the skin. While turning the fillets, be gentle in order to avoid breaking them.

For plating, spread a generous spoonful of artichoke purée on the bottom of the plate. I suggest that you use a bowl or a deep plate. Plate the roasted artichoke over the purée, and top it with the turbot fillet. On top of everything, sprinkle a little of the leftover orange zest, and finish with the deep fried artichoke and fried parsley leaves.

RISOTTO ZUCCA, SALVIA E GORGONZOLA

pumpkin, sage and gorgonzola cheese risotto

SERVES: 4 | PREPARATION TIME: 45 MINUTES | COOKING TIME: 1 HOUR

As with every great risotto, to prepare this traditional Northern Italian recipe, the key is to select good quality ingredients, starting with the rice. Proudly humble products like arborio rice from *Riso Gallo* and pumpkin come together with rich creamy gorgonzola cheese to create this extremely oozy and sumptuous dish. The aromatic note of sage and the acidity of white wine gives the risotto a beautiful depth of flavour. This dish is a fantastic vegetarian option, always a must in all my buffet and gala menus from September to the end of the festive season.

1.5kg pumpkin

Salt and pepper, to taste

2 tbsp extra virgin olive oil

2 cloves garlic, smashed

80g onion, finely chopped

280g Riso Gallo Arborio rice

100ml prosecco DOC

1 litre vegetable or chicken stock

50g creamy gorgonzola cheese, roughly chopped

20g Grana Padano, grated

10g unsalted butter

1 small bunch of sage, for garnish

Preheat the oven to 120°C.

Cut a small part of the pumpkin into small cubes and set aside.

You will need 60g of pumkin purée. For this, cut the rest of pumpkin into slices, season with salt and pepper, drizzle over some oil and add the garlic. Put the pumpkin on a baking tray covered with kitchen foil and roast in the oven for 30-40 minutes. When cooked, the pumpkin should be very soft. Discard the garlic and blend in a food processor until smooth.

Gently fry the chopped onion in a small casserole dish with a drizzle of extra virgin olive oil and a pinch of salt for about 10-15 minutes on a low heat, until golden and caramelised. Set aside.

In a large casserole dish, start to roast the rice on low heat with a pinch of salt, without adding oil or fat. This way, the heat reaches the core of each rice grain resulting in a more uniform al dente texture. Keep stirring the rice so it does not catch on the bottom of the pan and burn. When the rice is very hot, pour the prosecco DOC in. Let the alcohol evaporate, set the cooking time to 15 minutes and add the stock a ladle at a time, little by little. Stir the rice occasionally, and keep cooking.

Halfway through the cooking time, add the onion to the rice, along with the pumpkin cubes and the pumpkin purée.

Once the time is up, taste the risotto and if you're happy with the texture remove it from the heat.

This step is called mantecatura, making the risotto creamier and increasing its natural ooziness with the right gestures and movements.

Add the gorgonzola, the Grana Padano and butter to the rice. Stir with energy to incorporate extra air until the risotto is nice and creamy. Season to taste.

Plate the hot risotto straight away and garnish with the sage leaves and some extra gorgonzola.

RISOTTO CON CIPOLLA CARAMELLATA, QUAGLIA E TARTUFO ESTIVO

braised onion risotto with roast quail and summer truffle

SERVES: 4 | PREPARATION TIME: 2 HOURS 15 MINUTES | COOKING TIME: 1 HOUR 20 MINUTES

This is one of the most successful signature dishes I have ever done. To use the words of food critic, William Sitwell, this dish was to him "utter perfection." It transforms a classic risotto into an elegant dish to be served at a gala dinner as the main star of the menu. I always use the best rice for this risotto, which for me is the *Carnaroli Gran Riserva* rice by *Riso Gallo*. The onion is caramelised, which gives great sweetness to the dish, beautifully paired with chard asparagus and roast quail. Quail is a very delicate meat, but when served pink and accompanied by summer truffle, it is sumptuous. This may appear as a complicated dish, but by taking time and following the recipe carefully, it is easily achievable and extremely rewarding.

4 large quails

FOR THE QUAIL SAUCE

Quail trimmings

1 carrot

1 onion

1 celery

1 clove garlic

1 small bunch of herbs (rosemary, thyme)

20g unsalted butter

1 tbsp extra virgin olive oil

50ml dry white wine

500ml dark veal stock

80g summer truffle

Salt and pepper, to taste

FOR THE RISOTTO

10g dry porcini mushrooms

1 bunch green asparagus

3 tbsp extra virgin olive oil

300g onions, roughly chopped

280g Carnaroli Gran Riserva rice Riso Gallo

100ml prosecco DOC

1 litre chicken stock

1 small bunch of thyme

1 clove garlic

40g Grana Padano, grated

30g unsalted butter

Start by trimming the quail. Make sure there are no large feathers and with the help of a blow torch, slowly burn the skin of the quail to remove any excess of broken feathers. Remove the breasts from the carcasses. Set the breasts aside, piling one on top of the other for each quail (skin side out). Keep the legs for another dish, and save all the other trimmings for the sauce.

Start preparing the sauce. In a saucepan, roast the quail trimmings on high heat with all the chopped vegetables, garlic, herbs, a knob of butter and a drizzle of extra virgin olive oil. Roast well until golden and dress with a pinch of salt and pepper. Pour the wine into the saucepan and let the alcohol evaporate. Add the veal stock and let it simmer. The liquid should reduce by two thirds. Once ready, pass the liquid through a fine sieve. Keep to one side. Clean the summer truffle thoroughly and grate finely. Add to the sauce. Set aside.

Powder the dry porcini in a blender and set aside. Trim the asparagus, peel them and chop into segments. Roast in a non-stick pan until coloured. Remove from the heat and dress with a drizzle of extra virgin olive oil and a pinch of salt and pepper. Set aside.

Now move onto the onion. Gently sweat the onion in a casserole dish with a drizzle of extra virgin olive oil and a pinch of salt and pepper. This should take about 20 minutes on low heat. Keep cooking until well caramelised and soft. Add a ladle of stock to the onion. Once well cooked and browned, blend in a food processor until smooth. Keep the sweet onion purée aside.

Next, start to roast the rice on low heat with a pinch of salt without oil. The heat will reach the core of each rice grain better, resulting in uniform al dente texture. Keep stirring the rice and once very hot, pour the prosecco into the pan. Allow the alcohol to evaporate and set the cooking timer to 15 minutes. Add the stock little by little, keeping it simmering. Stir the rice occasionally. When half the time is up, add the onion purée to the risotto and keep stirring. While the rice is cooking, heat a non-stick frying pan with a drizzle of extra virgin olive oil, a couple of thyme stalks and crushed garlic clove. Gently roast the quail paired by breasts. Each side should cook for about 2 minutes, until golden. Dress with salt and pepper and set aside.

Once the risotto cooking time is over, taste the risotto and if you're happy with the texture, remove from heat and start with the mantecatura, which is how you make the risotto creamier, increasing its natural ooziness with the right gestures and movements. Add the Grana Padano and the butter to the risotto and stir with energy until creamy. Season to taste. Serve into hot plates. Garnish with the asparagus, creating nests for the quail breasts. Sprinkle with dry porcini powder. Present the quail and summer truffle sauce on the side and finish the plate in front of guests.

SAN PIETRO CON ASPARAGI BIANCHI E TARTUFO NERO

john dory with white asparagus and black winter truffle

SERVES 4 | PREPARATION TIME: 30 MINUTES | COOKING TIME: 20 MINUTES

This recipe is a match made in heaven. I usually prepare this dish for gala dinners as it is a sure-fire way to really impress guests. The John Dory is a flat white fish, like a lemon sole, turbot or brill. It is a very flavoursome and meaty fish, which is also tender, making it beautiful paired with asparagus and black winter truffle.

Ask your fishmonger to fillet the fish for you, as it is quite difficult to do.

16 large white asparagus

150g white onion, finely chopped

2 tbsp extra virgin olive oil

2 white potatoes

50ml double cream

10g Grana Padano, grated

Salt and black pepper, to taste

400g John Dory, filleted

20g unsalted butter

1 small bunch of thyme

50g black winter truffle, washed and dried

Remove the bottom woody part of the asparagus stalk. With the help of a potato peeler, peel the skin off the asparagus from the top to the bottom. Leave the tip untouched. Rinse the asparagus under water, and boil in salted water for 2 minutes. Cool them in iced water to retain their texture and colour.

Sweat the onion in a casserole dish with a drizzle of extra virgin olive oil, the thyme and a pinch of salt until golden. Peel and finely chop both the white potatoes, and roughly chop half of the asparagus. Remove the thyme and add the asparagus, potatoes and the double cream to the casserole dish, and keep cooking for 10 minutes.

Add the Grana Padano and blend everything. Pass through a fine sieve to obtain a smooth asparagus purée and season to taste with salt and black pepper.

Sprinkle the fish fillets with salt and pepper. In a non-stick pan, cook the fish with a drizzle of extra virgin olive oil on a high heat for 2 minutes on each side of the fillet, until golden.

Remove the fish from the pan. Proceed to fry the leftover asparagus in the same pan with the unsalted butter. Season with salt and pepper. Start plating with a generous spoonful of asparagus purée on the bottom of the plate. Gently place the cooked asparagus on the purée and top with the John Dory fillet. Finish the dish with plenty of grated winter truffle.

AGNELLO ALLA LIQUIRIZIA CON PESTO DI FAVE, CICORIETTA E PALLOTTE CACIO E OVO

lamb with liquorice sauce, broad bean pesto, wild chicory

SERVES: 4 | PREPARATION TIME: 2 HOUR 30 MINUTES | COOKING TIME: 1 HOUR 30 MINUTES

FOR THE LIQUORICE SAUCE
500ml dark veal stock
Lamb trimming
1 onion
1 carrot
1 celery stalk
1 garlic clove
1 small bunch of rosemary
20g butter
1 tbsp extra virgin olive oil
Salt and pepper, to taste
100ml white wine
20g liquorice, unsweetened

FOR THE WILD CHICORY
400g wild chicory
1 shallot, chopped
1 tbsp extra virgin olive oil
20g unsalted butter
15g sultanas
Salt and pepper, to taste

FOR THE BROAD BEAN PESTO
500g cooked broad beans, skin removed
4 tbsp extra virgin olive oil
1 small bunch of mint
1 small bunch of basil
100g pecorino cheese, grated
100g Grana Padano cheese, grated
½ clove garlic
Salt and pepper, to taste

FOR THE GARNISH
1 onion
1 tbsp extra virgin olive oil
Pinch salt and pepper
2 tomatoes, chopped
1 red pepper, chopped
8 pallotte cacio e ova, (see page 66)
40g red pickled onions, (see page 219)
1 small bunch of marjoram

FOR THE LAMB LOIN
2 lamb loins
Salt and pepper, to taste
10g unsalted butter
1 clove garlic
1 small bunch of rosemary
1 tbsp extra virgin olive oil

This main course is a signature dish of mine. I love cooking lamb, as it is a traditional meat used in *Abruzzo* that I learnt how to work with growing up. The idea of pairing the intense balsamic flavour of liquorice sauce with lamb is a recent discovery for me. It has been successful ever since, with two Michelin-starred chef Marcus Wareing describing it as "an unexpected combination of very clever cookery." This recipe combines the tender lamb loin with the freshness of a broad bean pesto and the bitterness of wild chicory, all served with the crispy bread and cheese balls with tomato and pepper purée.

Make sure the lamb loin is trimmed. Using a paring knife, carefully cut around the loin of the lamb and remove all excess fat and tough tissue. Save the trimmings and bones for the sauce. Put the loin aside.

For the sauce, chop the trimmings and roast them with all the vegetables and herbs together with butter and extra virgin olive oil. Add a pinch of salt and pepper, and cook until golden. Add white wine and allow the alcohol to evaporate. Add veal stock to the pan. Allow to simmer and reduce by half. Add the liquorice.

Once it has reduced to about half of its original size, pass through a fine sieve. Leave on the stove to simmer and reduce further to obtain a thicker consistency.

For the chicory, rinse under cold water. Separate the leaves from the stalk and remove the yellow damaged leaves. Boil the leaves and stalk separately in salted boiling water. The leaves will cook for approximately 2 minutes, whereas the stalk will require 4-6 minutes. Once cooked, leave in iced water to retain colour. Drain and mix together. In a pan, sweat the chopped shallot with extra virgin olive oil and a pinch of salt. Once caramelised add the butter, drop the chicory into the pan and stir well. Set aside.

Pre-soak the sultanas.

For the pesto, take the pre-cooked broad beans and blend in a food processor with all the other ingredients until it creates a rough, grainy paste. Set aside at room temperature.

For the garnish, start by sweating the onion in a casserole dish with extra virgin olive oil and a pinch of salt and pepper. When caramelised, add the tomatoes and red pepper. Let it cook for approximately 10-15 minutes. Blend it to create a smooth sauce, and pass through a fine sieve. Keep warm.

For the lamb loin, preheat the oven to 180°C and season the meat with salt and pepper. Sear the loin along the edges in a hot pan with a drizzle of extra virgin olive oil. Once golden, which should take a couple of minutes, add a few cubes of butter, a garlic clove and rosemary. Remove from the pan, and bake for 2 minutes in the oven on a baking tray.

Meanwhile, fry the pallotte cacio e ova in oil. Start plating a quenelle of broad bean pesto on the side of the plate. Place the wild chicory with the sultanas on the opposite side of the plate. Sprinkle sea salt flakes on the chicory. Garnish with the tomato and pepper purée with the pallotte cacio e ova and pickled red onions. When the meat is ready, allow to rest for 1 minute. Slice and place in the middle.

Top with a spoonful of liquorice sauce, and garnish with marjoram leaves.

TAGLIATA DI MANZO CON PUREA DI CAVOLFIORE E PESTO DI BASILICO E AGLIO SELVATICO

beef tagliata with cauliflower purée, wild garlic and basil pesto

SERVES: 4 | PREPARATION TIME: 2 HOURS 15 MINUTES | COOKING TIME: 1 HOUR 15 MINUTES

This sophisticated main course is ideal for a special or formal meal. It may not seem so Italian, but it originates from the traditional *Tuscan* beef *tagliata*. A rare beef steak grilled and sliced, the original recipe calls for it to be simply served with rocket and cherry tomatoes. However, I created my own version of this dish boasting a delicious assortment of flavours from ingredients I have come across since moving to the UK. The beef jus is optional when serving as the dish will work just as beautifully without.

FOR THE BEEF JUS

Beef trimmings (from rib eye)
1 onion
1 carrot
1 celery stalk
1 clove garlic
1 small bunch of herbs (e.g. rosemary, thyme)
1 tbsp extra virgin olive oil
20g butter
500ml dark veal stock
100ml white wine

FOR THE CAULIFLOWER PURÉE

1 large cauliflower
80g onion, chopped
1 tbsp extra virgin olive oil
100ml double cream
60g Grana Padano cheese
10g unsalted butter
Salt and pepper, to taste

FOR THE BEEF

2 X 300g thick beef rib eye steaks
Salt and pepper, to taste
1 clove garlic
1 sprig rosemary
4 baby shallots
4 baby artichokes, pickled (see page 64)
2 tbsp extra virgin olive oil
16 baby Swiss chard leaves
10g unsalted butter

FOR THE MUSHROOM POWDER

40g dried porcini
10g vegetable ashes
50ml dry white wine
1 tbsp of extra virgin olive oil
Salt and pepper, to taste

TO GARNISH

40g wild garlic and basil pesto (see page 216)
Sea salt flakes, to taste

For the beef jus, start by trimming the edge off the rib eye steak, removing the tough connective tissue around the meat, but keeping a thin layer of fat. Set the steaks aside to start preparing the sauce.

Peel and roughly chop the vegetables, and keep the trimmings to make the vegetable ashes. These will be used later for the mushroom powder.

In a saucepan, roast the beef trimmings with all the vegetables, garlic and herbs, extra virgin olive oil and butter with a pinch of salt and pepper until golden. Pour in the wine, allow the alcohol to evaporate. Add the veal stock and let it simmer. The liquid should reduce by half. Pass it through a fine sieve, and reduce it further depending on your preference of thickness.

For the cauliflower purée, wash the cauliflower and cut roughly. Boil in salted water for approximately 5 minutes until well cooked. Meanwhile, in a casserole dish, sweat the onion with a drizzle of extra virgin olive oil and a pinch of salt. Once the onion is soft, drop the cauliflower into the casserole dish. Add a ladle of cooking water. Leave it to cook. Once soft, put in a blender. Add the double cream, Grana Padano cheese and butter into the blender. Blend well until smooth and without lumps. Set the purée aside.

For the beef, season the meat with salt and pepper. Rub with rosemary and garlic to add more flavour. Cut the shallots and artichokes in half. Roast them well in a frying pan with a drizzle of extra virgin olive oil, and a pinch of salt and pepper. Blanch the Swiss chard leaf quickly and cool in iced water.

For the burnt porcini mushroom powder, put all the vegetable trimmings on a baking tray and cook at 200°C until well burnt. Powder them in a blender. Then proceed to powder the dried porcini in the blender. Combine the porcini powder with some of the vegetable ashes.

Ideally, the beef should be cooked in a barbecue, but if one is not available, a non-stick pan will do. On a high heat, seal the meat with a drizzle of olive oil on each side until golden. For a rare steak, cook for 3 minutes each side. Glaze the meat with a knob of butter and leave it to rest for a couple of minutes.

Now prepare to plate the dish. Spread a spoonful of cauliflower purée on the plate. Arrange the vegetables around it. Cut the meat into thick slices. Arrange the meat on top, finishing it off with sea salt flakes. Add the garlic and basil pesto. Sprinkle the porcini powder on top and if you are using, dress with beef jus.

GUANCIALINO DI VITELLO ALLA PIZZAIOLA
veal cheeks pizzaiola

SERVES 4 | PREPARATION TIME: 1 HOUR 30 MINUTES | COOKING TIME: 3-4 HOURS

Tender veal cheeks braised in a tomato pizzaiola sauce using only the best passata from *Imperiale d'Abruzzo*; it's rich, naturally sweet and one of my favourite signature dishes. The Ambassador loves it too, making it great for any occasion.

This dish screams Italy!

650g veal cheeks

Salt and pepper, to taste

500ml Imperiale D'Abruzzo Passata di Datterini

4 tbsp Imperiale D'Abruzzo extra virgin olive oil

10g dry oregano

Small bunch basil

20g flour, for dusting

1 celery stalk

2 carrots

2 garlic bulbs

1 large white onion

50ml white wine

300ml chicken stock

1 small bunch of mixed herbs (bay leaves, thyme, rosemary, basil)

FOR THE POTATOES

2 large yellow potatoes

2 tbsp Imperiale D'Abruzzo extra virgin olive oil

FOR THE CHICORY

500g green chicory (or green dandelion)

1 shallot, chopped

20g unsalted butter

1 tbsp Imperiale D'Abruzzo extra virgin olive oil

10g raisins

Trim the cheeks with a small knife and remove all the excess fat and connective tissue. Marinate them with salt and pepper for 30 minutes.

In a separate bowl mix the passata tomato sauce with 2 tablespoons of extra virgin olive oil, oregano, basil, salt and pepper. Do not blend it.

Dust the cheeks with flour and in a large pan heat the remaining olive oil and start cooking the meat for 5 minutes on each side at a high heat until golden. Turn down the heat to medium, remove the cheeks and in the same pan, fry the vegetables with garlic and onion. Pour in the wine and stock and season with salt and pepper.

Put the cheeks back in the pan, make a bouquet garni (use the herbs to make a bundle tied together with string) add it to the pan and leave to cook with the lid on for 2 hours, checking and turning the cheeks regularly.

After 2 hours check the cheeks – if they are soft and nearly falling apart that means they are ready. Gently remove them and place them aside. Strain the cooking liquid into a clean pan, add the pizzaiola sauce and let it cook for 15 minutes on a medium heat. Now add the cheeks back in the sauce assuring they are well covered. Keep it simmering for at least 5 more minutes to let them absorb all the flavour.

Meanwhile, boil the potatoes, peel them and mash them. Dress with abundant extra virgin olive oil and season with salt and pepper to taste.

Wash the green dandelion, blanch it in salted boiling water for 3 minutes and cool it in iced water to retain the colour. Strain it and gently fry in a pan with the chopped shallot and butter.

Dress the plate with the chunks of veal cheeks in the middle, a nice spoon of potatoes and some dandelion with the raisins on top. Finish off with an extra spoon of pizzaiola sauce and a drizzle of olive oil.

To take it to the next level you could add black olive powder, dried ground capers and deep fried crispy parsley leaves.

MOUSSE ALLO YOGURT CON ALBICOCCHE CARAMELLATE E CRUMBLE AL PISTACCHIO

yoghurt mousse with caramelised apricot and pistachio crumble

SERVES: 4 | PREPARATION TIME: 1 HOUR 15 MINUTES (PLUS SIX HOURS IF MAKING PISTACHIO SPONGE) | COOKING TIME: 20 MINUTES

This light, summery dessert is perfect for fruit lovers, combining delicacy and acidity by pairing creamy yoghurt mousse with the sharpness of apricot.

For the more audacious, this dish can be brought to a different level with tangy fresh herbs and fresh chilli.

FOR THE PISTACHIO CRUMBLE

100g unsalted butter, softened

100g ground pistachio

100g 00 flour

100g sugar

FOR THE YOGHURT MOUSSE

6g edible gelatine leaf

200g plain white yoghurt

150g whipping cream

80g icing sugar

FOR THE APRICOTS

4 large apricots

150g brown sugar

FOR THE PISTACHIO SPONGE (OPTIONAL)

40g pistachio paste

40g sugar

100g eggs

12g 00 flour

TO GARNISH

1 small bunch of fresh basil

2 tbsp pistachios, chopped

Start with the crumble. Make sure the butter is at room temperature then combine all of the ingredients in a mixing bowl. Knead well, and leave the dough to rest for 20 minutes. Roll the dough out with a rolling pin until it forms a 1½cm thick layer. Bake in the oven at 180°C for 10 minutes until golden. Let it cool down and break into pieces to obtain a crumble.

Now prepare the yoghurt mousse. Soak the gelatine in cold water. In a small saucepan, gently heat a couple of spoonfuls of yoghurt. Do not bring to the boil. When hot, remove from the heat and put in a mixing bowl. Add the pre-soaked gelatine to the hot yoghurt and allow to melt. In a separate bowl, whip the cream with icing sugar. Once the yoghurt with gelatine has cooled down, add the rest of the yoghurt and fold the whipped cream in gently. Mix well and let it rest in the fridge for 1 hour.

Now prepare the apricots. Remove the stones from two apricots, and use for the purée. Cut the apricots roughly and put in a saucepan with a couple of spoons of brown sugar. Cook on low heat until the sugar is melted and the apricots are soft. Remove from the heat and blend until it creates a purée. Pass through a fine sieve if necessary.

To make the optional pistachio sponge, combine all ingredients into a blender. Blend until smooth. Pour the mixture into a cream whipper. Close tightly and attach two bulbs. Let it rest in the fridge for 6 hours. To make the sponge, take a plastic cup and pierce a hole on its base with a sharp knife. Shake the cream whipper well and whip the mixture into a plastic cup. Fill half of the cup. Cook in the microwave at maximum power for 30 seconds. Remove from the microwave, and remove the sponge from the plastic cup.

To caramelise the apricots, cut the other 2 apricots into wedges, and sprinkle evenly with brown sugar. Caramelise the glazed apricots with a kitchen torch or under a grill. Proceed to plate the dessert. First, put some crumble and apricot purée. Add two generous quenelles of the yoghurt mousse and the caramelised apricots. Finish with some pistachio sponge if you have made it and garnish with chopped pistachio and fresh basil.

PANNA COTTA ALLA ZUCCA CON MELE E MOSTO COTTO

pumpkin panna cotta with apples and mosto cotto

SERVES: 4 | PREPARATION TIME: 2 HOURS (PLUS TIME FOR SETTING) | COOKING TIME: 40 MINUTES

Growing up in Italy, I was never a fan of panna cotta. As a chef, I use to regard it as a very basic recipe and therefore not very attractive. It never quite stood out, yet it was offered in many restaurants. However, after arriving in London, I discovered how fashionable panna cotta can be. Despite it being a simple recipe made with just a few ingredients, it is very challenging to get the panna cotta's wobble factor just right. Its hidden beauty is that it can be paired with various ingredients and flavours. Today, I make a pumpkin panna cotta, using the natural sweetness of the pumpkin paired with apples and the acidity of *mosto cotto* (translated as "cooked must") from producers *Imperiale d'Abruzzo*. This has since become a signature dish of mine.

FOR THE ALMOND CRUMBLE

100g sugar

100g unsalted butter

100g ground almonds

100g 00 flour

FOR THE PUMPKIN PANNA COTTA

1 pumpkin

125ml milk

250ml double cream

25g sugar

10g edible gelatine leaf, soaked

FOR THE APPLES

3 large pink apples

60g sugar

1 small bunch of fresh thyme

1 unwaxed lemon

20g butter

4g cinnamon

20ml Imperiale d'Abruzzo mosto cotto

Start with the almond crumble. In a large mixing bowl, knead all the ingredients together well until they create a smooth dough. Let it rest at room temperature for 30 minutes. With a rolling pin, roll out 1cm thick sheet. Line a tray with baking parchment and cook the sheet at 170°C for approximately 10-12 minutes until golden. Allow to cool. Once cool break it into crumble pieces and leave aside.

For the panna cotta, start with the pumpkin purée. You'll need 150g for this recipe; any extra purée can be kept aside and used as an accompaniment for pasta, risotto, or meat. Remove the skin and seeds from the pumpkin and cut into rough pieces. Put the pumpkin pieces in a glass bowl and cover with cling film. Cook in the microwave for 10-12 minutes at maximum power. Once cooked, the pieces should be really soft. Put the pieces into a food processor and blend until smooth. Once ready, remove the pumpkin purée and drain over a fine sieve to remove the excess water. The purée will retain a stronger flavour by doing so.

In a saucepan, combine the milk, cream and sugar and bring to a simmer. Once hot, remove from the heat. Melt the pre-soaked gelatine into the hot mixture and pour the pumpkin purée in, reserving some to garnish the plate. Mix well and allow to cool down for a few minutes. Pour the panna cotta into small moulds. Leave the moulds in the fridge to set for 2-3 hours.

Now, prepare the apples. Start with the apple brunoise. Take one apple, trim and remove the seeds. Do not discard anything while doing so, set aside. Cut small cubes and dress with a couple of spoons of sugar, a few thyme leaves and a drop of lemon juice. Set aside. Now prepare the caramelised apple purée with the two remaining apples. Remove the skin, trim them, and remove the seeds. Cut into rough cubes and cook in a frying pan with a knob of butter, two tablespoons of sugar, a drop of lemon juice and cinnamon. Roast until caramelised all around. Remove from the heat and put the caramelised apples into the food processor. Blend until they create a smooth purée. Set aside to cool down.

Put all the apple trimmings into the food processor, add a glass of water, the leftover sugar and lemon juice. Quickly blend well and remove from blender. Pass through a fine sieve. Let it drain slowly. This will create an apple consommé, similar to an apple juice.

Take a pasta bowl to plate. Spread a teaspoon of pumpkin purée as a base. Remove the panna cotta carefully from its mould by using a palette knife and add to plate. Garnish with the apple brunoise and a nice quenelle of apple purée. Top with almond crumble and finish the plate by glazing the panna cotta with a teaspoon of mosto cotto. In front of guests, add a generous spoon of apple consommé and enjoy.

TIRAMISÙ AL CIOCCOLATO
chocolate tiramisu

SERVES: 4 | PREPARATION TIME: 3 HOURS | COOKING TIME: 30 MINUTES

This dessert is my take on the classic tiramisu, with an added twist of chocolate. It's a fairly new creation of mine, but has been a success since I showcased it on BBC MasterChef: The Professionals. In the words of Marcus Wareing: "A classic and simple Italian dessert brought into the modern world." For the more adventurous, I suggest putting some hazelnut into the tiramisu to add further texture.

FOR THE COFFEE ICE CREAM

4 egg yolks

150g sugar

150ml milk

100ml espresso

150ml double cream

2g ice cream stabiliser

FOR THE COCOA CRUMBLE

125g flour

80g unsalted butter, at room temperature

40g caster sugar

25g cocoa powder

FOR THE COFFEE GELATINE

100ml espresso

20g sugar

5g edible gelatine leaf

25ml coffee liqueur

FOR THE MASCARPONE MOUSSE

4 egg yolks

100g sugar

6g edible gelatine leaf

100ml sweet wine (Passito or Moscato)

250g mascarpone

50g whipping cream

FOR THE CHOCOLATE GANACHE

80g egg yolk

35g sugar

150ml double cream

100ml milk

150g dark chocolate (55%)

4g edible gelatine leaf

Start with the coffee ice cream. Whisk the egg yolk with sugar. Separately, warm the milk, coffee and cream together and pour them on the eggs mixture. Make sure everything is well combined. Put on the stove on a low heat until you have reached 80°C (use a kitchen thermometer), and cool immediately. Once the mixture is cold, pour it into the ice cream machine. Once it is ready, after approximately 30 minutes, place in a container and leave to rest for around 2 hours in the freezer.

To prepare the cocoa crumble, which will be the base of the dessert, make sure the butter is at room temperature and roughly chopped. Knead all ingredients until it creates smooth dough. Wrap in cling film and leave to rest in the fridge for around 30 minutes. Preheat the oven to 180°C. With a rolling pin, roll the dough out to form a 2cm thick sheet. Bake in the oven for 12 minutes. Once the crumble is cooked, let it cool. Break the dough into rough pieces. Set aside a few pieces of crumble to use later as a garnish. Use the crumble as a base for the chocolate ganache.

For the coffee gelatine, boil the coffee with sugar. Soak the gelatine in cold water. Once the coffee is hot and the sugar has melted, remove from heat. Drain the gelatine, squeezing to remove any excess water. Drop into the coffee. When the gelatine has cooled down add the coffee liqueur.

For the mascarpone mousse, use a mixer to whisk the egg yolks with the sugar until the mixture becomes pale white. Meanwhile, soak the gelatine in cold water. Separately, bring the sweet wine to boiling point. At this stage, when the wine is hot, squeeze the gelatine and allow it to melt in the wine. Pour the hot wine into the egg mixture, as if pasteurising the egg yolk with the hot wine. Let it cool. Once cool, fold the mascarpone in. In a different bowl, whip the cream. Fold the cream with mascarpone and egg mixture to create a light and soft mousse.

For the chocolate ganache, the centrepiece of the dessert, beat the egg yolk with sugar. In a saucepan, mix the cream and milk and bring to boiling point. Pour the hot mixture into the egg yolk and sugar. Whisk thoroughly and put the mixture back onto the heat. Meanwhile, break the chocolate into pieces and soak the gelatine leaf. Let the mixture reach 80°C using a thermometer then remove it from the heat and pour the hot mixture onto the chocolate. Mix until well melted and smooth. Squeeze the pre-soaked gelatine leaf in cold water and add into the hot chocolate ganache.

Once the chocolate ganache cools down, but is still liquid, pour onto the crumble in the moulds. Let it cool in the fridge for a couple of hours. Make sure there is space on the surface of the mould, to later add the coffee gelatine. Once the ganache has set, gently reheat the coffee gelatine and drop a spoonful of it on top of the ganache. Return to fridge for 15 minutes minimum.

Put the chocolate ganache on the plate and garnish with the mascarpone mousse on top with the help of a piping bag. Dust with cocoa powder and serve the ice cream on the side, or in a separate bowl.

MERINGATO CASTAGNE E CIOCCOLATO
Chocolate and chestnut meringue

SERVES: 6 | PREPARATION TIME: 2 HOURS 45 MINUTES (PLUS OVERNIGHT TO SOAK THE BORLOTTI BEANS AND 6 HOURS TO REST FOR THE SPONGE CAKE) | COOKING TIME: 45 MINUTES

This signature dessert of mine is a bit more complex than others in this book and the key ingredient, chestnuts, might not be to everyone's taste, but it happens to be one of my favourite fruits. Growing up, I spent lots of time with my grandparents in a small mountainous village where we would collect chestnuts from our family trees and roast them in our fireplace. By mixing sweet and savoury ingredients I wanted to recreate an earthy edge in my chestnuts dessert, a dish that still reminds me of the walks in the woods with my granddad.

FOR THE CHOCOLATE AND CHESTNUT GANACHE

80g egg yolk
35g sugar
100ml milk
150ml double cream
150g dark chocolate (55%)
150g boiled chestnuts
30g brown sugar
50ml water

FOR THE HAZELNUT SPONGE

40g sugar
40g hazelnut paste
100g egg
12g 00 flour

FOR THE BEAN CRUMBLE

100g borlotti beans powder
50g 00 flour
1 egg
30g butter, softened
25g muscovado sugar

FOR THE ITALIAN MERINGUE

250g sugar
50ml water
125g egg whites
Pinch salt

OTHER INGREDIENTS

200g roasted chestnuts, roughly chopped
160ml coffee gel (see page 198)
Coffee powder, to dust

To make the powdered beans first soak the borlotti beans overnight. The following day, rinse the beans and place in a saucepan full of water. Bring to the boil. Do not add salt or sugar to the water. Once cooked, drain the beans and place them on a baking tray. Let the beans dry in the oven at 100°C for 2-3 hours. Powder the beans in a powerful blender. This step can be prepared in advance and the dried beans can be stored.

Add a couple of spoons of coffee gel into pasta bowls to create a thin layer and let them set in the fridge for a couple of hours. Now prepare the chocolate and chestnut ganache. Beat the egg yolk with the sugar until it creates a pale mixture. Meanwhile, warm the milk and cream in a pan. Pour the hot mixture on top of the egg yolk with sugar. Whisk well and put the mixture back on the heat. Allow the temperature to reach 80°C with the help of a kitchen thermometer. Break the chocolate into rough pieces into a mixing bowl. Proceed to slowly pour the hot mixture onto the chocolate and mix well until smooth. Put the boiled chestnuts in a saucepan with the sugar and water. Bring to the boil and mash the chestnuts with a spoon while the saucepan is warm. Then move to a blender, and blend until it becomes a chestnut purée. Combine the chocolate ganache with the chestnut purée. Set aside to cool down. Once cool, put the mixture into a piping bag.

Now move onto preparing the hazelnut sponge. If you do not have hazelnut paste, it is easily made by blending hazelnuts in a food processor until it reaches a paste-like consistency. Combine all ingredients in a blender. Blend until smooth. Pour the mixture into a cream whipper. Close tightly and attach two bulbs. Let it rest in the fridge for 6 hours. To make the sponge, take a plastic cup and pierce a hole on its base with a sharp knife. Shake the cream whipper well and whip the mixture into a plastic cup. Fill half of the cup. Cook in the microwave at maximum power for 30 seconds. Remove from the microwave, and remove the sponge from the plastic cup.

To make the borlotti beans crumble, combine all the ingredients together into rough pieces into a large mixing bowl. Knead well until it creates crumble-like dough. Line a tray with baking parchment and spread the bean crumble. Bake at 160°C for about 8-10 minutes until golden. Allow the crumble to cool down. It should easily break.

Now make the Italian meringue. Combine the water with the sugar and bring to the boil. With the help of a thermometer, allow the temperature to reach 121°C. It will create a syrup. Meanwhile, in a large mixing bowl whip the egg whites with a pinch of salt until firm and foamy. Once the syrup has reached 121°C, pour it slowly onto the whipped egg whites. Keep mixing the egg whites while pouring the syrup, until the meringue has become warm. Allow to cool. Once cool, put into a piping bag.

Remove the bowls with the gelatine layer from the fridge. Add a few drops of chocolate and chestnut ganache, as well as some roughly chopped roasted chestnuts. Top with some crumble, and dust with coffee powder.

Break the halzenut sponge into rough pieces, and add to the bowls. Then top with some Italian meringue drops. To finish, flame the meringue with a kitchen torch for it to caramelise. Serve immediately.

LA DISPENSA
Breads, sauces, condiments and basics

Though the title of this chapter translates as 'pantry', this section not only refers to store cupboard staples like sauces and condiments, but other recipes that will come in useful time and time again, like bread, pickles and types of pasta.

This section embodies the Italian approach to cooking, about reusing ingredients and not wasting or throwing anything away. For instance vegetables that aren't at their freshest anymore can be pickled, and stale bread can be made into crisp breadcrumbs.

You'll save money by making your own bread and condiments, but more than that you'll gain a sense of satisfaction after making something for yourself. Seeing a loaf rise and grow in front of you is a wonderfully simple pleasure. I guarantee it will taste better because you made it.

It reflects my view of cooking; that it's not just about feeding people, but something from which you can obtain joy.

CIABATTA SENZA IMPASTO

ciabatta

SERVES: 4 | PREPARATION TIME: 15 MINUTES (90 MINUTES OF PROVING) | COOKING TIME: 20 MINUTES

This is an extraordinarily easy recipe resulting in rustic *ciabatta* bread that is crunchy on the outside and really soft inside. This method is known as *ciabatta* "without mixture" because it doesn't require any kneading at all. What makes this recipe special is the high quantity of water compared to the flour amount. Give it a try!

6g yeast

200g strong bread flour

190ml water

4g chestnut honey

4g salt

Melt the yeast, whisking it in warm water, then roughly mix all the ingredients with a rubber spatula. The dough shouldn't be smooth, but rough and grainy.

Leave to rest for 1½ hours in a warm place, mixing every 30 minutes with the spatula.

Preheat the oven to 230°C. Line a baking tray with baking parchment and dust with a lot of flour. Gently place the dough on it making sure it falls in the middle. Bake at 210°C for 20 minutes until brown and crunchy outside.

Cool the ciabatta over a wire rack to avoid extra humidity.

GRISSINI STIRATI

grissini

MAKES: 120 GRISSINI | PREPARATION TIME: 1 HOUR (PLUS TIME TO PROVE) | COOKING TIME: 6 MINUTES

With a little patience everybody can make these wonderful fragrant extra virgin olive oil *grissini*. It is a very simple and traditional recipe from *Piedmont* in north west Italy. The *grissini* can be stored for over 10 days. *Stirati* translates as "pulled" as the dough should be flexible and the grissini are pulled when you make them to give them an extra long shape.

16g fresh yeast

265ml water

500g 00 flour

80g Manitoba flour

90ml extra virgin olive oil

15g table salt

4g sugar

1 tbsp honey

Durum flour, for dusting

First melt the yeast in the water. Knead all ingredients together until the dough is smooth and elastic. Once the dough is ready, shape into five logs. Put on a baking tray lined with baking parchment. Allow space for each log, and place onto the tray. Keep the logs separate by using layers of parchment paper between each one. Brush the logs with extra virgin olive oil. Leave to prove for approximately 1½ hours at room temperature.

Once the proving time is over, sprinkle durum flour on the working surface. Carefully remove each log, as to avoid removing the air accumulated during the rising. One at a time, place each log onto the working surface. With a flat pastry spatula, cut each log into small grissini. Gently pull each grissini by its extremities (this is called "stirare"), creating a long grissino. Fold the two opposite ends underneath the edge of the baking tray. Repeat for each grissino until all the dough has been used.

Gently trim the overlapping end of each grissino with a knife or pizza cutter. Preheat the oven to 205°C. Bake the grissini for 5-6 minutes, until golden and crispy. Let them cool down and either serve immediately or keep in an airtight container for approximately 10 days.

STREGHETTE EMILIANE AL ROSMARINO

emilia-style crispy flatbread

MAKES: 3 BAKING TRAYS | PREPARATION TIME: 90 MINUTES | COOKING TIME: 10 MINUTES

This dish is from *Emilia Romagna*, which is a very gastronomically renowned region, and not only for salumi and cheeses. This rosemary flavoured crispy flatbread made of flour, yeast, water and extra virgin olive oil will undoubtedly impress your guests.

Traditionally lard is used in this recipe, but I prefer a mix of extra virgin olive oil and a bit of butter. Make them a day in advance and keep them in air tight container.

250g 00 flour

125ml water

12g fresh yeast

15ml extra virgin olive oil (plus extra to brush)

10g unsalted butter, room temperature

6g salt

1 small bunch of rosemary, chopped

Salt flakes, to garnish

Knead all the ingredients (except for the rosemary and salt flakes) well until you have a smooth and compact dough. Cover with a cloth and leave to rest for at least 1 hour at room temperature.

Once the dough has risen, divide the mixture in four pieces without working the dough too much. Sprinkle some flour over the working surface and using a pasta machine or a rolling pin roll the dough into 2mm thin sheets.

Preheat the oven to 200°C.

Cut the dough with a crimping wheel into rough squares or any shape you like and place on an extra virgin olive oil greased baking tray. Brush the flatbread with oil on top as well, scatter over some sea salt flakes and rosemary and bake at 190°C for 7-8 minutes until golden brown.

FOCACCIA ALL'OLIO EXTRA VERGINE DI OLIVA

extra virgin olive oil focaccia

SERVES: 6 | PREPARATION TIME: 40 MINUTES (PLUS 4-5 HOURS OF PROVING) | COOKING TIME: 22 MINUTES

This is my favourite *focaccia* recipe ever. It is not too difficult to make and works wonderfully with rosemary, fresh cherry tomatoes and oregano. Soft, fragrant and delicious served warm, though if you really want to treat yourself, stuff it with *Culatello di Parma*.

Remember, with every bread recipe the secret is time, so allow it time to rise two or even three times; it will really make the difference.

15g yeast

75ml extra virgin olive oil

460g 00 flour

40g Manitoba flour

15g salt

150g cherry tomatoes

1 garlic clove, chopped (optional)

25g black olives from Cerignola

250ml water

Sea salt flakes, to taste

1 small bunch of rosemary

Melt the yeast in warm water and knead with olive oil, both flours and salt until the dough is smooth and uniform. Add the salt when the yeast is completely melted to avoid yeast lumps. Leave the dough to prove for 1½ hours at room temperature in a bowl dusted with flour – remember to cover with a tea towel.

When the dough has doubled in size work it on the table taking out all the air and leave it to rest for another 1½ hours.

After this roll out the dough with a rolling pin until 3cm thick and place it on a baking tray folded with baking parchment. Cut the cherry tomatoes and sprinkle them over the focaccia with the garlic and the rinsed black olives, drizzle over some extra virgin olive oil and leave to rise for an extra 1½ hours.

Preheat the oven to 220°C. After the last proving, bake the focaccia for 10 minutes at 210°C. Sprinkle with some water, turn down the temperature to 180°C and bake for another 12 minutes, placing a bowl of cold water on the bottom of the oven to create the right amount of humidity for the focaccia. Once crispy and golden take the focaccia out of the oven and sprinkle straight away with sea salt flakes and freshly chopped rosemary.

Serve warm.

PANINI ALLE OLIVE
green olive breadrolls

MAKES: 30 SMALL BREAD ROLLS | PREPARATION TIME: 1 HOUR (PLUS 6 HOURS OF PROVING TIME) | COOKING TIME: 10 MINUTES

These little fragrant sour dough rolls with green olives are an ideal meal accompaniment.

They can also be served as a traditional afternoon snack with a slice of *salame* (cured meats).

FOR THE DOUGH

16g fresh yeast

250ml water

200g 00 flour

50g Manitoba flour

18g salt

1 tbsp honey

6g sugar

100g pitted green olives (from Cerignola)

250g flour, for second kneading

1 egg white

For the dough, melt the yeast in the water. Slowly add all the other ingredients (except for the olives, flour for dusting and egg white) and mix in a bowl until the dough is smooth, even if still "watery". Cover with cling film and let it prove for at least 2 hours at room temperature. After proving time, knead the dough with 250g of flour, and chopped green olives. Knead well until the dough is smooth and elastic. Cover with a tea towel and let it rest in a bowl for 2 hours. After this proving time, dust the dough with flour on a flat surface and cut in 30g pieces. With the palm of your hand, roll the pieces into small balls. Prepare a baking tray and line with baking parchment. Place the small bread rolls onto the parchments, allowing a few centimetres between each one. Dust a little flour on the dough, lightly mark each bread roll with a knife and let them prove for another hour. Be careful with the temperature of your room, if too hot they will rise much more quickly. The rolls should double in size.

Preheat the oven to 220°C. Place a bowl of water in the bottom of the oven to create humidity. Cook the bread rolls at a minimum of 210°C for approximately 5 minutes. Quickly remove them from the oven and brush the rolls with egg white wash. Return to the oven. Cook at 180°C for an extra 2 minutes until the rolls are slightly golden all over.

PANINI AL LATTE
milk bread rolls

MAKES: 30 BREAD ROLLS | PREPARATION TIME: 1 HOUR | COOKING TIME: 10 MINUTES

A very easy and useful recipe for really soft bread rolls. You can keep in the fridge for few days sealed in a plastic bag and warm them up as you need them.

I love them with a slice of Parma ham, or you can use less salt and add more sugar for the perfect sweet buns.

25g fresh yeast

300ml milk (plus extra to brush)

550g bread flour

50g softened butter

20g salt

30g sugar

1 egg yolk, to brush

Melt the yeast in the milk at room temperature. It's important to not add the salt before the yeast is completely melted to prevent yeast lumps. Add all the ingredients together and knead well until the dough is smooth and elastic.

Leave the dough to rest at room temperature for about 2 hours until it has doubled in size. With a spatula cut pieces of dough around 30g and with the palm of your hands form them into small round rolls, like ping pong balls. Place them as you go on to a baking tray folded with baking parchment. Brush the rolls with a bit of milk and leave them to prove for 40 minutes.

Preheat the oven to 230°C, brush the rolls with the yolk and bake for about 6 minutes at 220°C with a small bowl of water on the bottom of the oven to create some humidity. When they are nice and golden rest assured, it means they're well cooked!

PASTA MULTICOLORE
multi-coloured pasta

SERVES: 8-10 | PREPARATION TIME: 1 HOUR 30 MINUTES (PLUS 4-5 HOURS FOR RESTING) | COOKING TIME: 1 MINUTE

After having made the multi-coloured *tortellini* on MasterChef: The Professionals, it soon became a signature dish of mine. It is an easy technique once you get the hang of it, but it requires practise and time. The technique shared in this recipe can be applied to various ingredients to create lots of coloured pasta, from black squid ink to red tomato paste. A good start is the pink, yellow and green pasta below. The recipe allows you to play with ingredients and fresh pasta to create beautiful *ravioli*, *tortellini* or *tagliatelle*. The pasta block can be stored in the freezer if it is not used right away.

FOR THE YELLOW PASTA

2 fresh Italian yellow eggs

200g 00 flour

FOR THE GREEN PASTA

1 small bunch of parsley

2 fresh eggs

200g 00 flour

FOR THE PINK PASTA

2 fresh eggs

20g cooked beetroot

1 tsp beetroot juice

240g 00 flour

OTHER INGREDIENTS

Durum flour, to dust

For the yellow pasta, knead the egg with the flour until it makes a smooth and elastic dough. You only reach the right consistency if the pasta has been worked hard enough to allow the gluten molecules to break down; the dough's elasticity is very important for the final result. Wrap in cling film and let it rest for 30 minutes.

For the green pasta, blanch the parsley leaves in salted boiling water. Cool in iced water to retain their colour. Blend the cooked parsley with the eggs. Knead the egg mixture with the flour until smooth and elastic. It should have the same consistency as the yellow pasta. Wrap in cling film and let it rest for 30 minutes.

For the pink pasta, blend the beetroot well with the beetroot juice and the egg. Knead the pink egg mixture with the 00 flour until elastic and smooth. If a pasta is too dry, add a bit of egg. If the pasta is too wet, add a little flour. Wrap in cling film and let it rest for 30 minutes.

Roll out 3 sheets of the same thickness through the pasta machine for each colour. The thickness of the sheet will correspond to the thickness of the coloured stripe. Once all the pasta doughs have been rolled out, proceed to stack the coloured sheets on top of each other. Make sure that there is no flour caught between the layers. Cut the layered block in half. Stack the second half on top of the first block. This process can be repeated if necessary. Wrap the block in cling film and let it rest in the fridge for approximately 4-5 hours. This pasta works beautifully when making filled pasta, such as tortellini or ravioli. To obtain a beautiful striped ravioli, cut a thin slice of pasta from the block. Roll it out lengthways once or twice through the pasta machine: the stripes should be perpendicular to the pasta machine. Following this procedure, you can create all sorts of beautiful shaped pasta.

PESTO AL BASILICO E AGLIO SELVATICO
basil and wild garlic pesto

SERVES: 4 | PREPARATION TIME: 15 MINUTES

A great condiment made from humble ingredients in just a couple of minutes, the versatile basil pesto is good to dress salads, meats and fish and is perfect with pasta. The *Ligurian* tradition calls for all raw ingredients to be pounded and crushed together with a pestle and mortar until creamy, however you can make your life easier and use a food processor.

My personal touch to this recipe is to add a bit of wild garlic when in season. Remember to use fresh Italian basil and good extra virgin olive oil; it will really make the difference.

50g basil leaves, washed and dried

10g green wild garlic leaves

40g Grana Padano, grated

90g Imperiale D'Abruzzo extra virgin olive oil

12g pine nuts, toasted

Salt and pepper, to taste

Put all the ingredients in the container of your blender or food processor and place it in the fridge for 30 minutes. The cold temperature will help retain the natural green colour of the basil. Blend together for about 30 seconds until creamy. Use it fresh or store in a glass jar for no longer than 2 weeks in the fridge.

SALSA VERDE
green sauce

MAKES: 2 JARS | PREPARATION TIME: 20 MINUTES | COOKING TIME: 10 MINUTES

Salsa verde is one of my favourite relishes. This is a traditional recipe from the northern region of *Piedmont*, but it is so popular that it has become a classic of Italian cuisine. This famous condiment made by parsley, mint and extra virgin olive oil was traditionally served with *bollito misto* (mixed boiled meat) but it works really well with any fish or vegetables, or you can simply serve it as dipping sauce with a selection of antipasti. Very aromatic, *salsa verde* adds a refreshing burst of flavour to any dish.

You can use a pestle and mortar to pound and crush all the ingredients together, but a food processor will do the job as well. Once done you can store your salsa verde in the fridge in an airtight jar for 2 weeks.

80g parsley leaves, picked

30g fresh mint leaves, picked

1 sliced white bread, slightly stale

200ml white wine vinegar

15g capers

2 anchovy fillets

1 clove garlic, peeled

3 green olives, pitted

30g pine nuts

1 hardboiled egg, yolk

2 small gherkins, pickled in sweet vinegar

120ml extra virgin olive oil

Salt and pepper, to taste

Wash and dry the parsley and mint leaves. Cut and put the bread in a small bowl, add the vinegar and leave it for a few minutes to soak.

After rinsing the capers and draining the anchovies, put them in the mortar and add the parsley, the mint and the garlic clove.

Pound them in a pestle and mortar until you achieve a paste consistency. Add the pitted olives, pine nuts, the squeezed soaked bread and pound again.

Add the yolk, the gherkins and the extra virgin olive oil whilst pounding constantly.

Add salt and pepper to taste, but be careful with the salt as some of the ingredients are already quite salty.

CONSERVE & CONDIMENTI

ESTATE 2016

CARAMELLO SALATO
salted caramel

MAKES: 1 JAR | PREPARATION TIME: 10 MINUTES | COOKING TIME: 15 MINUTES

Caramel sauce is a really versatile building block for dozens of desserts, and making your own caramel is a simple process. You can pair it with fresh creamy desserts like panna cotta or drizzle over chocolate cake. Even if you only need a small amount, make a whole jar and store in a cool dry place for months.

The most popular version made with fresh cream is salted caramel, which I simply love coming through in the background of a chocolatey dessert. However you can make sweeter flavoured versions (just leave out the salt) by mixing coffee or fruit juices with the cream. Remember if your caramel gets too thick, add a bit of cream and warm it up together.

120g sugar
200ml fresh cream, warmed
50g softened butter
10g salt

In a heavy-bottomed saucepan start to melt the sugar over low heat, stirring with a wooden spoon if necessary.

When it starts to brown in spots, swirl it occasionally just to even out the color, and keep the hot spots from burning. It shouldn't be too dark, more of a golden amber. The darker you go, the more bitter and complex the flavour gets, however you don't want to take it so far that it tastes burned.

When your caramel is medium amber, you've reached the optimum colour and consistency. Remove it from the heat and pour in some warmed cream. Be careful because the sugar will bubble and spurt when the cream is added and it might dry off quickly.

Return the pan to the heat until the cream is incorporated and the caramel is completely melted.

At this stage take it off the heat, let it cool for a couple of minutes and incorporate the softened butter, stirring continuously to avoid the butter splitting. Now incorporate the salt and pour the caramel in a sterilised jar until needed.

MAIONESE
infallible mayonnaise

MAKES: 2 JARS | PREPARATION TIME: 10 MINUTES | COOKING TIME: 10 MINUTES

Nobody wants to go through the pain of whisking their own mayonnaise by hand, so it's always tempting to reach for the store-bought alternatives. Believe me though, you'll never have anything as good as a fresh homemade version – it's just not possible! This easy recipe contains a little trick that will change all the rules of your cooking. It's perfect to use for a wonderful vitello tonnato sauce.

2 eggs
10g mustard
1 large lemon, squeezed
10ml white vinegar
40ml extra virgin olive oil
Salt and pepper, to taste
400ml sunflower oil

The key to this recipe is to slightly pasteurise the eggs, not only for your safety but for the right consistency of the mayo.

Boil the eggs for just 1½ minutes and cool them down immediately in iced water.

Open the eggs in a bowl, making sure to catch all the cooked egg white stacked on the inside of the shells with a teaspoon. Add the mustard, lemon juice, vinegar, extra virgin olive oil, a pinch of salt and some freshly ground pepper.

Blend with a hand mixer and gradually pour the sunflower oil until thickened. Make sure to incorporate all the oil with the mixer but do not stir too much while blending to avoid tearing the sauce apart.

CIPOLLA ROSSA DI TROPEA IN AGRODOLCE
pickled tropea red onion

MAKES: 2 JARS (250ML EACH) | PREPARATION TIME: 15 MINUTES | COOKING TIME: 10–15 MINUTES

I love pickling vegetables, especially the red onion from *Tropea*, in Italy. It is a particular onion that grows only in *Calabria*, around the town of *Tropea*, from which it takes its name. It has a stronger flavour and is much sweeter in taste and aroma than other red onions. It is not as red as the others, but it is perfect to make jams with. Its sweetness is one of the reasons why I love to pickle this particular onion. It can be preserved for months, and is a great accompaniment for meat, fish and in salads.

Tip: Add a few drops of beetroot juice to the pickling liquid to get a darker red colour.

3 Tropea red onions
1 litre water
150ml red wine vinegar
1 bay leaf
20g sugar
10g salt
6 peppercorns
1 tbsp beetroot juice (optional)

Peel the external part of the onions and cut them into halves. Remove the centre of the onion and keep for other preparations as it can be very strong in flavour. Cut the onion in strips, no larger than 1.5cm. Put into a pot with the water, vinegar, bay leaf, sugar, salt and peppercorns (and optional beetroot juice). Bring to boiling point and allow to simmer for 10 minutes until the onion softens. Remove from the heat and let it cool down in the cooking liquid. Pour into a sterilised glass jar and store it in a cool dry place.

SALSA POMODORO
tomato sauce

SERVES: 6 | PREPARATION TIME: 10 MINUTES | COOKING TIME: 30 MINUTES

Every Italian family will tell you that they possess the secret to the perfect tomato sauce. To me, there are no secrets behind a tomato sauce. You should rely solely on good ingredients, and treat them with respect. Follow simple steps, and you will make a great sauce, which can be used in any dish, from pasta to fish. No secrets, no fuss, just simple good ingredients. Good passata can be found all year round, but it is always better to use fresh tomatoes when they are in season.

1 white onion
4 tbsp Imperiale d'Abruzzo extra virgin olive oil
Salt and pepper, to taste
1 small bunch, fresh basil
2 black olives
1 garlic clove, chopped
½ chilli
600g Imperiale d'Abruzzo passata di pomodoro

Chop the onion roughly. In a large casserole dish, sweat the onion with the extra virgin olive oil and a pinch of salt. Cook until they start to caramelise, this will bring out all the lovely sweetness of the onion. Once the onion is done, add basil, the olives and garlic. Cook for a couple of minutes. Add half a chilli. When the onion, garlic and basil are golden, pour the passata in. Add an extra pinch of salt and black pepper. Let it simmer for 15 minutes. A good tomato sauce does not need to be cooked for hours, no more than 30 minutes. The tomato sauce should become thicker, having been reduced by a third. Once cooked, it can be used straight away, or put into sterilised jars to be used to dress pasta or as sauce for fish and meat. Before serving make sure to remove the cooked basil and substitute for a few fresh leaves.

CHEF'S TIPS

I recommend the use of extra virgin olive oil. It is more expensive but you will taste the difference. It is always worth investing money in your ingredients – just be more careful with how you use them.

Where possible, always take the fresh option rather than frozen and use dry pulses instead of the canned, making sure you soak them overnight beforehand.

Try to seek out seasonal ingredients. Don't make a tomato salad in December, or if you do don't expect it to be great.

You should strive to use local products – I know in the UK there are lots of imported ingredients, and not just Italian, however imported does not always mean better. You cannot avoid imported products and ingredients altogether in my recipes as some require it, but always check to see if there is a local alternative first.

Gather as much knowledge of what you eat as possible; it's important to know where your meat, fish and vegetables have come from.

I always deep fry in vegetable oil and never in extra virgin olive oil, not only because it is cheaper, but also because I find it lighter in taste.

Always fry in clean oil. Use the right amount and then dispose of it.

Truffles are expensive but you don't need to use much and if you stick to seasonal varieties they can be cheaper. Make sure you always clean them, even if it is not stated in the recipes.

In recipes with garlic and onion, make sure you peel them first, even if they are not to be chopped.

Some ingredients can be exchanged for similar ones and the recipe will still work: e.g. pumpkin for butternut squash, romanesco cauliflower for broccoli. Use imagination and do not panic if you can't find exact ingredients – be creative.

Always be extra careful with raw fish or marinated fish – don't have raw fish if you haven't frozen for at least 24 hours prior at -20°C, and always defrost thoroughly before use.

For fresh pasta try to use Italian or rich yolk eggs as they have larger, brighter and tastier yolks. I'm not sure whether this is because they're corn-fed or whether it's because English chickens don't get as much sun, but trust me they are much more flavoursome.

I always recommend using fresh herbs. You'll find they give a different depth of flavour to the dishes will require the use of less salt and condiments.

As with every bread recipe (and most of the cakes), try to use always a small percentage of strong flour in with the rest.

Try always to make your own stock and don't rely on overly processed dry ones. Often all it takes is a cheese crust and a few vegetables bubbling away for 30 minutes.

On some recipes I use a dark veal stock which is a basic ingredient that can be found in most delis and some supermarkets. If you prefer, you can make your own as you would a normal stock but with roasted veal bones instead of just boiled.

Never throw away shellfish trimmings, peelings or fish bones. You can use these to make a nice stock so pop them in the freezer for when you need it next.

Some people find it curious that in each risotto recipe I always use chicken stock – I find it's the most suitable compared to fish or vegetable stock as they both can result in a darker colour and stronger flavours, reducing during the cooking of the risotto.

When you are storing pickles, pesto or sauces, you must put into a sterilised jar, especially if you are keeping for more than a couple of days. To do this, boil them in water for a few minutes, and make sure you do the lids too. Fill them straight away. It is important to be safe, especially in home cooking!

When baking bread you need to allow yourself plenty of time – there is no quick recipe. Time to prove and rest is not optional, and should always be done at room temperature. You should also always save a piece of dough to be used the next time as a sourdough starter.

Always try to use fresh yeast rather than powder. Also, never mix the yeast with the salt before the yeast has melted otherwise it will form lumps.

In most of these recipes, I always recommend you preheat the oven to a higher temperature than you need, and then turn to the correct one once the food is in the oven. This is because many domestic ovens lose their heat very quickly when the door is opened.

By sweating the onion, I mean slowly cook them until they get rid of their own vegetable water.

Always save homemade bread, grissini and focaccia. They will make fantastic coarse breadcrumbs.

Whenever you are baking, remember the bigger the cake or bread is, the longer it will take to cook. Lower the temperature and keep cooking.

4 Grosvenor Square

©2016 Meze Publishing & Danilo Cortellini.
All rights reserved.

First edition printed in 2016 in the UK.

ISBN: 978-1-910863-19-0

Written by: Rachel Heward

Photography by: Marc Barker

Edited by: Phil Turner, Paul Cocker

Designed by: Paul Cocker, Marc Barker,
Matt Crowder

PR: Kerre Chen

Printed by Bell and Bain Ltd, Glasgow

me:ze
PUBLISHING

Published by Meze Publishing Limited
Unit S8-S9 Globe Works
Penistone Road
Sheffield S6 3AE
Web: www.mezepublishing.co.uk
Tel: 0114 275 7709
Email: info@mezepublishing.co.uk